IT'S LEVEL UP TIME!

Gaming has never been so fun. This year has seen exciting technological developments in the gaming industry. From advancements in cloud gaming to artificial intelligence, these trends are reshaping the gaming experience as we know it by offering greater accessibility, immersion, and graphics. It is the year of high-quality game releases, with new titles such as *Star Wars Jedi: Survivor* and *Legend of Zelda: Tears of the Kingdom* proving super popular, and remastered games also having their moment.

Level Up is your go-to guide for these games and more. With the tips and tricks inside this book, you'll have all you need to beat any game of your choice, and who knows, you might even find a new favorite!

STAY SAFE AND HAVE FUN!

■ Games are wonderful, but you need to know how to stay safe while you're playing, especially when you're playing online. Follow these simple rules to have a great time!

1 Talk to your parents and agree on some rules about which games you can play, when you can play them, and whether you can play them online.

2 Never give out any personal information while you're gaming, including your real name, where you live, your parents' names, where you go to school, any passwords, or your phone number. Never agree to meet someone you've met online or through a game in person. As much as possible only play games with people you know IRL.

3 Tell your parents or a teacher if you come across something online that makes you feel uncomfortable.

4 Be nice to other players, even when you're competing against them. Don't say anything that might hurt someone's feelings or make them feel bad.

5 Take regular breaks when you're gaming. Give your eyes, hands, and brain a rest, and get your body moving.

6 Don't download, install, or stream any games without checking with your parents. Pay attention to the age ratings on games—they exist to protect you from content that might upset or disturb you, or that your parents won't be comfortable with you experiencing.

7 If you play mobile games outside, be aware of your surroundings. Don't play them alone and don't wander around the neighborhood without your friends or family.

2025 LEVEL UP

Writer:
Eddie Robson

Design, Editorial, and Project Management:
Dynamo Limited

ISBN 978-1-5461-2272-2
10 9 8 7 6 5 4 3 2 1
24 25 26 27 28
Printed in the U.S.A. 40
First printing, September 2024

CONTENTS

16

58

42

78

90

114
130
148
160
204
180

THE BIG GAMES

102 **Princess Peach: Showtime!**

168 **Final Fantasy VII Rebirth**

Whatever games or types of games you love, we want to help you level up! Read on and find out all you need to know about the biggest and best games of the last twelve months—and the ones you really don't want to miss! We're here with the skills and techniques to help you take on any challenge, from fighting to solving puzzles. Along the way, we'll also tell you how to build your own gaming PC, point you toward the best free-to-play and mobile games, and much, much more. So, what are you waiting for? Let the fun begin...

94 **Ride 5**

126 **Days of Doom**

64 **Wild Hearts**

THE 30 GREATEST GAMING MOMENTS

There's a lot to pack in as we look at the latest in gaming!

30

ROBLOX COMES TO PLAYSTATION Roblox

■ Roblox is home to some of the world's most popular games, but for the longest time it was only available on PC, iOS, Android, and Xbox. At the end of 2023, that changed as it was launched on the Meta Quest and then, finally, PlayStation. Thanks for sorting that out, guys—now, when's the Switch version coming?

29

FIVE NIGHTS AT FREDDY'S GOES FOR A NIGHT AT THE MOVIES

Five Nights at Freddy's

■ The team behind the *Five Nights at Freddy's* movie started work as soon as the game became popular. It took a few years to get the movie off the ground, but it was worth the wait, becoming the low-budget horror hit of the year. It captured what fans love about the games, right down to the Springlock suits!

28

IT'S TEKKEN AWHILE
Tekken 8

■ The latest in the *Tekken* series arrived nine years after *Tekken 7* hit arcades, and it adds another insanely overdramatic layer to the ongoing saga. For a game that's mostly based around one-to-one unarmed combat, there is a lot going on here, but it adds spice to a battle when you know the bitter backstory!

27

THE ELEPHANT IN THE ROOM IS . . . MARIO!
Super Mario Bros. Wonder

■ The *Mario* games continue to bring the unexpected, but we didn't expect *Super Mario Bros. Wonder* to include a power-up that would turn him into an elephant. With all the gang usable as playable characters, they all have the chance to get their trunk on!

26

HANDHELD POWER IS ON THE RISE
Steam Deck

■ The Steam Deck has been a hit, but its weak battery life compared with the Switch is a problem (the same reason the Game Boy crushed the competition in the 1990s—Nintendo went for battery over performance). The launch of the Asus ROG Ally shows others are willing to rival the Steam Deck—but they still haven't cracked the battery issue. Whoever does will win this battle, we think!

25

GETTING STUCK DOWN A WELL HAS NEVER BEEN SO MUCH FUN
Animal Well

■ Developers are still doing amazing new things with retro styles. In *Animal Well* you take control of a blob exploring a labyrinth full of animals. It takes inspiration from *Metroid* and *Zelda*, and we've never seen pixel art look so atmospheric and creepy!

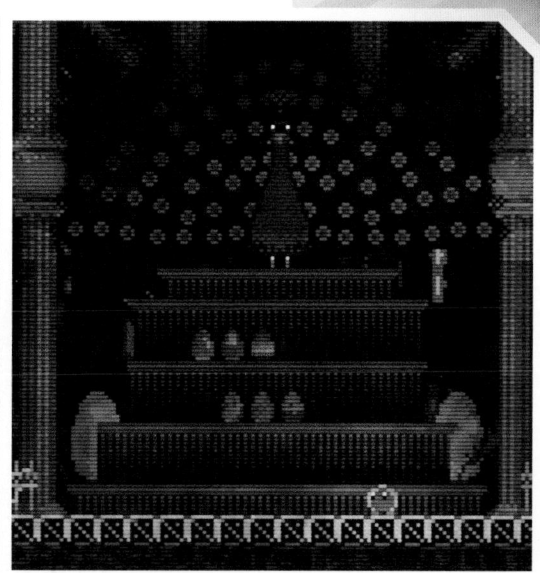

24

METROID IS BACK IN ITS PRIME

Metroid

■ There's no doubt *Metroid* is a classic series—there's a whole genre of gaming called "metroidvania" after it (and *Castlevania*). But it dropped off Nintendo's agenda during the Wii U era. That's all changed since they followed up 2021's *Metroid Dread* with a superb remaster of the GameCube's *Metroid Prime*. *Metroid* once again feels like a major Nintendo franchise!

23

FORTNITE BRINGS US ROCK AND ROCKETS

Fortnite

■ *Fortnite's Rocket Racing* crossover with *Rocket League* is actually more like *Mario Kart* crossed with *Daytona Racing*, and is tons of fun. Epic is moving into new genres in a big way, launching *Fortnite Festival* as a revival of games similar to *Rock Band* and *Guitar Hero* that were huge in the 2000s.

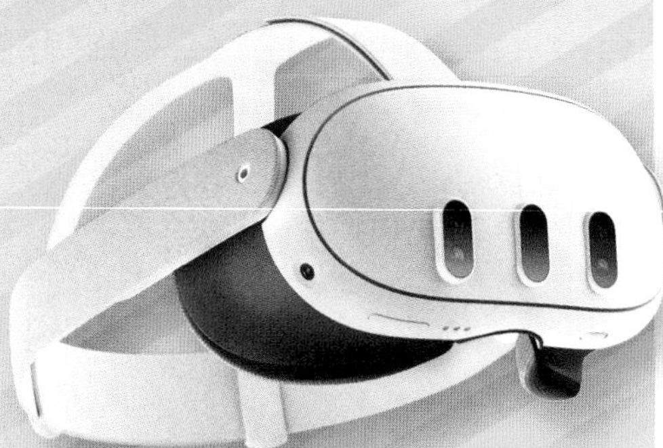

22

A NEW QUEST BEGINS

Meta Quest 3

■ It's been a quiet time for major new hardware, but the Meta Quest 3 stands out—it's a successor to the device launched as the Oculus Quest 2 in 2020. It's making a serious play to be the leading VR headset, with a new *Ghostbusters* game (*Rise of the Ghost Lord*) and access to Xbox cloud gaming.

21

HIDDEN DEPTHS IN POKÉMON'S DLC

Pokémon Scarlet and Violet

■ *Pokémon Scarlet* and *Violet* divided fans of the series by moving away from the traditional story-based gameplay and replacing it with an open world. This world is expanded further in the two-part DLC, *The Teal Mask* and *The Indigo Disk*, focusing on Area Zero—the best part of the base game!

STREET FIGHTER 6 GOES BEYOND THE STREETS

Street Fighter 6

■ The *Street Fighter* series has come a long way from its arcade roots, and *Street Fighter 6* went beyond the one-on-one fighting format to offer an open-world mode. But its big innovations might be in its accessibility options, which offer extra sound cues to help sight-impaired players judge where the opponent is and where a blow has connected!

20

19

MARIO KART'S BOOSTER PASS TAKES US AROUND THE WORLD

Mario Kart 8 Deluxe

■ *Mario Kart 8 Deluxe* is by far the most-owned game on the Switch—it has sold 57 million units, meaning about 43 percent of all Switch owners have a copy. So, instead of releasing a sequel, it was a smart move to offer waves of DLC. The game's forty-eight circuits have now been doubled to ninety-six, including all fourteen of the cities visited in *Mario Kart Tour*!

18

GAMERS FLOCK TO WEIRD INDIE TITLES

■ The creativity in indie games continues to amaze us, and Annapurna Interactive has published many of the best, including *Kentucky Route Zero, Donut County, Sayonara Wild Hearts*, and *What Remains of Edith Finch. Flock* is another awesome original, in which you play a flying shepherd gathering hover-sheep and other creatures!

17

BATTLES AND CO-OP ON THE COUCH

■ It felt like the entire gaming world went nuts for online multiplayer in recent years. So many games seemed to be entirely built around their online modes, as if they didn't want you to play any other way. But the joy of playing together in the same room has made a real comeback! Can we get it in the next *Splatoon* please, Nintendo?

16

MARIO CONQUERS THE MOVIES

The Super Mario Bros. Movie

■ We always knew there was a great movie in the *Mario* series, and *The Super Mario Bros. Movie* gave us everything we wanted, with a ton of references for fans to spot!

15

A PLAYSTATION CLASSIC IS REBORN

Final Fantasy VII

■ There's no shortage of amazing, epic open-world RPGs these days—we were still trying to get full completion on *Tears of the Kingdom* when *Final Fantasy VII Rebirth* dropped. This remake of the middle bit of the 1997 PlayStation game opens the world out to an insane degree. We need more hours in the day!

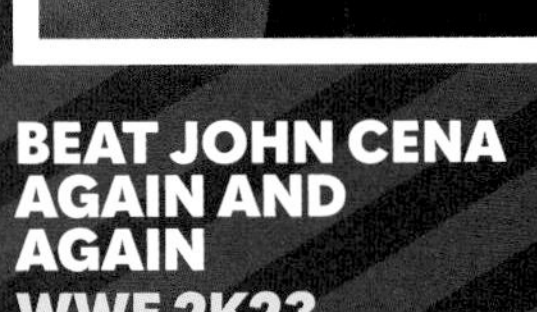

BEAT JOHN CENA AGAIN AND AGAIN

WWE 2K23

■ The big draw in *WWE 2K23* is its Showcase mode, featuring the game's cover star John Cena. While he is playable, in most of the Showcase matches you'll be playing against him. So actually, this mode is mostly about recreating Cena's most famous defeats, at the hands of opponents such as Rob Van Dam, the Undertaker, Triple H, and AJ Styles. It's pretty satisfying!

14

13

PRINCE OF PERSIA'S CROWNING GLORY

Prince of Persia

■ The biggest comeback came from *Prince of Persia*. The series went quiet a long time back, but *The Lost Crown* restored the classic gameplay we look for, in a gloriously designed world!

12 SONIC'S STAR IS ON THE RISE
Sonic the Hedgehog

■ *Sonic the Hedgehog* is bigger than it's been since the 1990s, with not only a third movie on its way, but also a spin-off *Knuckles* TV series, plus the games are smashing it on several fronts. There's *Sonic Superstars*, *Sonic Dream Team*, *The Murder of Sonic the Hedgehog*, and the official Roblox game continues to be updated. It's a great time to be a Sonic fan!

11 A SEA CHANGE IN THE RPG WORLD
Sea of Stars

■ In among the BIG, immersive 3D RPGs, indie hit *Sea of Stars* harked back to a simpler age with its SNES-style graphics and linear gameplay inspired by *Chrono Trigger* and *Super Mario RPG*. There's room for both types, and if you want an RPG you can finish in less than a month, *Sea of Stars* is the game for you!

9 PIKMIN BRINGS US A NEW DOG STAR Pikmin 4

■ *Pikmin 4* is the best since the original, and much of that is thanks to Oatchi. This faithful canine creature is the game's breakout star, a helper you can level up by teaching him new tricks. When they finally get around to making *Pikmin 5*, they surely have to bring this fellow back—or give him his own spin-off!

10 SPIDER-MAN WITH A HINT OF VENOM
Spider-Man 2

■ The *Spider-Man* games are doing an awesome job of putting together their own universe from familiar elements. Now they've got their own Venom, and in *Spider-Man 2* you get to play as him! Not for the whole game—just for a bit—but like Peter, once we've felt the power of Venom we can't help but want more...

8 WE DIG THE MINECRAFT TRAILS AND TALES UPDATE Minecraft

■ *Minecraft* continues to keep things fresh with regular updates, and the *Trails and Tales* update offers the rare cherry blossom biome and camels you can ride—but the real stroke of genius is the archaeology system. You can now find trail ruins containing suspicious blocks, which can be investigated to find precious pottery fragments!

GAMES ARE THE BEST VERSION OF STAR WARS RIGHT NOW 7
Star Wars Jedi: Survivor

■ While *Star Wars* takes a break from cinema, and the TV shows poke into the corners of the universe, the kind of epic storytelling we want from *Star Wars* can be found in video games. *Jedi: Survivor* has the scale and spectacular visuals of a movie, and it really feels like you're living in the *Star Wars* universe!

6 HER JOB IS PEACH
Princess Peach: Showtime!

■ Luigi's been given his own series. So have Donkey Kong and Wario. Yoshi has been the star of eleven games. Whereas Princess Peach has had just one game, 2005's *Super Princess Peach* ... until now! *The Super Mario Bros. Movie* recast her from helpless damsel in distress to a tough, capable leader, and in *Princess Peach: Showtime!* she's the star of the show—literally. She's having a moment!

5 REPRESENTATION FOR WOMEN'S SOCCER IS SLOWLY GETTING THERE

■ Video games generally do a very poor job of covering women's sport. The *FIFA* games started to correct this in *FIFA 16*, introducing international women's teams—then disappointed by coming back year after year with almost exactly the same small selection. *EA Sports FC 24* has improved further on these recent offerings and there are now seventy-four women's teams to choose from.

4

A HUMAN FINALLY BEATS TETRIS

Tetris

■ You can't complete *Tetris*, can you? Think again! Willis Gibson, a 13-year-old whose YouTube handle is Blue Scuti, played a 38-minute game in which he managed to hit level 157—not long ago *Tetris* experts thought the highest level a human could reach was 29—then the game froze and crashed. Gibson couldn't go any further!

3

A NEW PORTAL INTO YOUR PS5 PlayStation Portal

■ The PlayStation Portal is a genius bit of kit—it looks like a PlayStation version of a Switch, and it connects to your PS5 over Wi-Fi so you don't need a TV to play your games. It's not a full handheld, but it gives you the freedom to play your PS5 even if someone else wants to use the TV!

2

ZELDA HITS NEW HEIGHTS

Legend of Zelda: Tears of the Kingdom

■ *Breath of the Wild* was the best *Zelda* game in years, astounding fans with its expansive new open-world approach—so at first, the long-awaited sequel seemed a little underwhelming. It looked and felt like more of the same. But *Tears of the Kingdom* soon revealed just how ambitious it was. When you're leaping between floating ruins, dodging cannon fire from ancient robots, it doesn't feel like *Breath of the Wild* at all!

1

AN EPIC NEW ERA OF LEGO GAMES BEGINS

LEGO Fortnite

■ The *LEGO* games have been drifting a little since *LEGO Dimensions*, and their sandbox game *LEGO Worlds* got a mixed response. But they've come back in a big way, with a free-to-play *Minecraft*-style official *LEGO* game, set inside the world of *Fortnite*—and it's just the start of the collaboration between LEGO and Epic!

MARVEL'S SPIDER-MAN 2

SWINGING BACK ONTO YOUR PS5!

Spider-Man and its Miles Morales–starring glow up were a hard act to follow. The original wowed PlayStation gamers with its detailed open world mapped closely on the real New York City. No one had ever been able to step into the world of a Marvel superhero like this before. The reworked version placed a new story onto the same map, so no one expected anything too wild from it.

But where does the series go now? You don't want to take Spidey out of NYC—that's what makes these games great—so what's going to make it fresh? The answer, it turns out, is more New York...

QUICK TIPS

FAIRGROUND ATTRACTION

■ Go on all eight rides at Coney Island—saving the Speed Demon for last—you'll be rewarded with a choice of comedy hats and glasses!

MAIN FOCUS

■ Exploring an open world is fun, but if you focus on the story you'll unlock things faster.

STREET JUSTICE

■ If you see a crime, think: What would Spidey do? You'll be rewarded for stopping it.

NEXT GENERATION

■ *Miles Morales* was released on PS4 and PS5, but *Spider-Man 2* is exclusive to the PS5—and it makes great use of the newer console's power, with the city feeling even busier and more active than in the previous games.

SPIDER-MEN ASSEMBLE

■ The first game was mostly based around Peter Parker, while the remaster was led by Miles Morales. In this one, they work together. You can choose which to control while the other is CPU-operated. But it remains strictly a single-player game; there's no co-op.

A FIGHTING CHANCE

■ There was a lot going on in the combat system of the previous games, and you probably don't want to learn a whole new one—so you'll be glad to know combat isn't all that different.

QUITE A BITE

■ This time around the story concerns Kraven the Hunter and his private army, who hunt superheroes in NYC, and also the arrival of Venom, the alien symbiote, who bonds with Peter—which makes him a playable character, too …

REACHING OUT

■ Venom has his own moves, as you'd expect, and the gameplay transforms when you have his powers to work with and can achieve this kind of multi-enemy takedown. And this isn't the only variant Spidey suit in the game …

FAST FACT

In *Spider-Man: Across the Spider-Verse* you can see Miles's roommate Ganke Lee playing *Spider-Man 2* on his PS5 in their dorm room!

LIKE THIS? TRY THIS:

GOTHAM KNIGHTS

■ Another urban open-world superhero game, *Gotham Knights* is set in Batman's world—but the lead characters are the younger crimefighters Batgirl, Nightwing, Red Hood, and Robin, and you take them out for clue-finding and punch-ups.

GET ALL DRESSED UP

As anyone who's seen the *Spider-Verse* movies knows, Spider-Man comes in many different versions—and *Spider-Man 2* offers a total of sixty-eight variant costumes you can unlock. They're purely cosmetic, but as collectibles go, they're pretty great! In addition there are ten costumes—five each for Peter and Miles—available in the Digital Deluxe bundle. Some of these are *super* cool—and have some interesting references in their design . . .

If you look for the offices of lawyer Matt Murdock (aka Daredevil), which were in the original game, you'll find they're no longer there—and the developers have hinted this is setting up a plot element in the next game . . .

APUNKALYPTIC

The Spider-Punk suit you can unlock at level 26 is pretty great, but we think this one is even better. Of course, the dream is a game starring Spider-Punk from *Across the Spider-Verse*, but this will do for now.

STONE MONKEY

This suit designed by Victoria Ying is inspired by Chinese mythology and the tale of Monkey in the legend *Journey to the West*. The feathered cuffs and neck are wild!

AURANTIA

What's an Aurantia, you may ask. Well, it's a type of spider that can be identified by its yellow and black markings—which have been combined with Spidey's traditional red for this suit.

AGIMAT

The Agimat suit, which Miles wears, refers to a Filipino system of magic that uses charms known as agimats. Popular stories about this magic show people gaining superhuman strength, heightened senses, and the ability to generate electricity.

TOKUSATSU

The name of this Miles suit is a Japanese word meaning "special effects," which is also a genre of TV and movies in Japan—mostly fantasy and sci-fi. An example of tokusatsu is the highly popular Japanese Spider-Man series of the late 1970s, in which Spidey piloted a Gundam-style mecha.

THE LEGEND OF ZELDA: TEARS OF THE KINGDOM

NINTENDO MADE THE GREATEST GAME OF ALL TIME . . . AGAIN!

The long-awaited *Tears of the Kingdom* picks up the *Zelda* saga where the previous game, *Breath of the Wild*, left off—and when you first play it, it doesn't seem all that different. It looks the same, the basic mechanics are the same, even some of the music is the same—and it uses a modified version of the Hyrule map from *BotW*. Surely Nintendo wouldn't do a half-hearted job on a *Zelda* game?

But these fears quickly vanish, because *Tears of the Kingdom* introduces new abilities that completely change the experience and make you look at its world in a whole different way. And while *BotW* was one of the biggest games Nintendo had ever made, its successor is even bigger, adding a whole world in the sky and another underground!

QUICK TIPS

GET CREATIVE

■ Sometimes the game prompts you to use Ultrahand to solve a puzzle or make progress. But the option to use it is always there, and you can use your imagination. Check out this siege tower!

A HANDY SKILL

■ Link's new arm comes with some awesome skills. The first you'll learn is Ultrahand, which is the ability to move objects—and also to fix objects together and make new things out of them.

DO IT AGAIN

■ Later, you can pick up the Autobuild skill, which remembers things you've made before and lets you make it again if the pieces are nearby.

A GLOOMY SITUATION

At the outset, Link's arm is infected with Gloom, and Zelda vanishes... again. Fortunately when Link wakes up he's been supplied with a new arm by a ghostly being named Rauru.

LEARN THE ROPES

The adventure begins on the Great Sky Island, which is basically a massive tutorial that will probably take a few hours to play through. Make sure you stock up on cold-resistant dishes for the trip up the mountain!

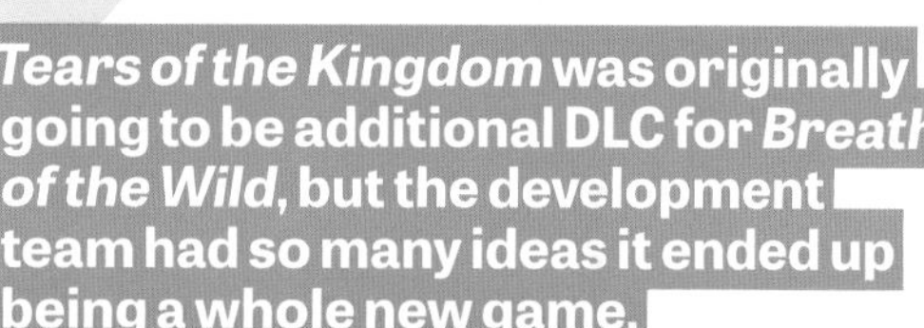

FAST FACT

Tears of the Kingdom **was originally going to be additional DLC for *Breath of the Wild*, but the development team had so many ideas it ended up being a whole new game.**

FEET ON THE GROUND

Once you get through that, you'll find yourself back in Hyrule—though it's devastated by the Gloom, and will feel different from when you last visited. And you'll need to fill in the map all over again...

DEEP, DEEP DOWN

If you head south of Lookout Landing, you'll discover the Depths—a whole new level to the world of Zelda. Proceed with caution and activate Lightroots, which can heal Gloom damage.

HEAD IN THE CLOUDS

But don't neglect the sky, because there's a whole world up there, too! It can be reached by using Skyview Towers and gliding, and there's a lot to find—rare plants, challenges, Shrines, Zonai Dispensers, and more.

LEFT TO YOUR OWN DEVICES

The prehistoric Zonai civilization is essential to the backstory of *Tears of the Kingdom*, and their lost technology is an important part of the game. Early on Link is given an Energy Cell that powers Zonai Devices, which pop up along the way.

CHARGE AHEAD

Soldier Constructs are scattered across the map, especially in high areas but also often in Shrines. When you defeat them they drop Construct Horns and Zonai Charges. The charges can be used to boost your Energy Cell—or you can save them . . .

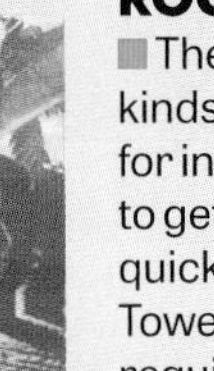

READY TO ROCKET

The devices have all kinds of uses—a rocket, for instance, can be used to get up to high places quickly. The Skyview Tower at Thyphlo Ruins requires you to do this in order to unlock it.

IN THE ZONAI

But you can also build with Zonai Devices, attaching them to other objects—including other Zonai Devices. These are the key to making your constructions come to life—rockets and fans are especially useful!

DISPENSING WISDOM

Put Construct Horns or Zonai Charges into Zonai Dispensers to get capsules containing devices. Putting in more charges will multiply the capsules you get back—one charge gives one device, but five charges get you twelve devices.

DO YOU RECALL?

Recall allows you to reverse the motion of an object. It can be difficult to understand the full potential of this skill at first, as it seems designed to work on specific puzzles. But there's a lot more to it.

FALL GUY

For instance, let's say you've run into something that's just fallen from the sky. You can't stand on it and use Ultrahand to travel up, because Ultrahand won't work on an object you're standing on.

TAKE IT BACK

But you *can* stand on it and then apply Recall to it. The object will return where it came from, with you on it. Always look out for falling objects and where you might ride them with Recall.

LEND A HAND

And if an object isn't moving, you can use Ultrahand to make it move, then bring it back… and *then* stand on it and use Recall on it. This can be used to make your own floating platforms to cross spaces!

LIKE THIS? TRY THIS:

TUNIC

If you don't have a Switch and crave some *Zelda*-style action, this cute indie adventure sees you play as a sword-wielding fox on a quest to free a spirit trapped in a crystal.

SAGE ADVICE

You can unlock even more abilities by completing the main quest in each region. You'll meet the Sages of Wind, Water, Lightning, Fire, and Spirit, and you can continue to call on their skills after the quest is done.

HIT BACK

Recall can even be used in combat. If you throw your sword at an enemy, use Recall to retrieve it. If an enemy flings a rock at you, use Recall to send it back and drop it on its head!

TEARS OF THE KINGDOM: WEAPONS AND FUSING GUIDE

A lot of the weapons are rubbish—make them better!

As in *BotW*, weapons break annoyingly quickly, though at least they have an excuse this time—the Gloom has corroded them. This means you need to constantly pick up new ones. Don't waste good weapons by using them on anything other than enemies. And always have a rock hammer you can use for mining. Here's our guide to being weapon-smart.

1 Look sharp

■ Royal Guard weapons are always a solid option. They deal extra damage with their last few hits before breaking, and they'll reappear in the place you found them after a Blood Moon. Moblin and Lizfalos arms do surprisingly good damage, but they're very fragile. Gloom weapons are effective but deal Gloom damage to the user. The unique weapons earned by defeating champions and completing quests don't last forever, but once found they can be purchased from Bargainer Statues.

FAST FACT

A live-action *Legend of Zelda* film is in development, directed by Wes Ball, who made the *Maze Runner* series of films. There's certainly a lot of lore for them to draw on...

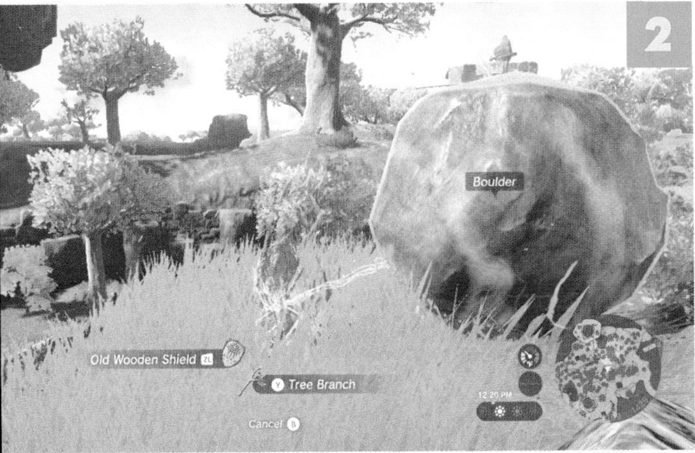

2 Put the "use" in fuse

■ For better weapons, you need to use Fuse. Early in the game you're taught how to use it to fuse weapons and objects to create new things—this is essential to keep yourself supplied with rock hammers. You can also get creative with it and create new weapons and implements. A shield fused to a Zonai cart makes an excellent skateboard, for instance. But there's an even more important way of using Fuse...

3 Toughen up

Monster parts in *BotW* weren't good for much except elixirs, but in *TotK* they're incredibly valuable because they make your flimsy weapons more durable. Fuse a monster horn or similar and you can double the number of hits a weapon can land before breaking. Be wary of wasting anything too valuable by attaching it to a weapon that'll break before long anyway, but basic monster parts should always be used to enhance your weapons.

4 Get to the point

More good news: unlike in *BotW* you don't have to carry multiple types of arrows, or remember which shops stock which types, because you can fuse almost any object to an arrow. Some won't do anything, but Fire Fruit and Ice Fruit will create fire and ice effects, while Bomb Flowers will create explosions, and Muddle Buds will cause enemies to turn on each other—great for tackling hordes of Bokoblins.

Tear away

Struggling to find all the Geoglyphs where the Dragon's Tears are located? After clearing the blizzard from Rito Village, meet Impa there to trigger a quest that will lead you to a map of all the Geoglyphs in the Forgotten Temple. Just remember to take a picture of it, because finding it won't mark the locations on your own map!

5 Eyes on the prize

Monster parts are also great to fuse with arrows. Elemental Chuchu Jelly can be used like Fire Fruit and Ice Fruit. Puffshrooms create smoke bombs. Gibdo bones increase damage. Wings make arrows fly straighter and farther—Keese wings are good, but Aerocuda wings are even better as they're resistant to wind. Eyeballs are best of all—an arrow equipped with one will home in on a target! And Keese eyeballs of the ice, fire, or electric variety also have that effect.

Disney Speedstorm

A kart racer filled with famous faces!

■ Just as *MultiVersus* is a free-to-play clone of *Super Smash Bros.* with characters owned by Warner Bros., so *Disney Speedstorm* is a free-to-play clone of *Super Mario Kart* with characters owned by Disney. Is this a trend? Will we see a free-to-play clone of *Mario Party* next year starring characters from whoever owns the Minions? Time will tell.

Given the enduring popularity of *Mario Kart*, it's surprising there haven't been more games serving that type of action to non-Nintendo (Nontendo?) platforms. And not only is *Disney Speedstorm* free, but it's also cross-platform. So whatever device you have, you can play it—and you can play it against others thanks to local and online multiplayer modes.

FAST FACT

The course named The Silver Screen sees you breaking through a cinema screen and into a world based on the early black-and-white Disney cartoons like *Steamboat Willie*—and there's an unlockable Steamboat Mickey character who has a unique skill of Happy Whistling.

The art of karting

■ The mechanics of *Speedstorm* will be familiar to anyone who's played *Mario Kart*. As you race you collect items from random gift boxes that can be used to attack your opponents. The flip-screen attack is especially nasty!

Drifting away

The drift control, where you skid into a corner and accelerate out of it, also comes from *Mario Kart*, but it's even more important here, because it charges your boost bar. This mechanic is specific to *Speedstorm* and is crucial to winning!

Changing the rules

There are different types of races, which demand different skills—ones where everyone must use the same type of power-up, ones where racers must jump to reach speed boosts and power-ups, elimination races, fogbound races, ones where only certain power-ups are valid for your racer…

Feel free

Of course, with it being free to play there are in-game purchases. At the start the only racer available is Mickey Mouse. Unlocking more requires you to make progress in the game and/or pay real-world money on passes and packs. Donald Duck can quickly be unlocked in free play.

The gang's all here

As well as the Mickey Mouse gang, the game includes playable characters from *Aladdin*; *Beauty and the Beast*; *Frozen*; *Hercules*; *The Jungle Book*; *Lilo & Stitch*; *Monsters, Inc.*; *Mulan*; *Pirates of the Caribbean*; *Toy Story*; and more!

AVATAR: FRONTIERS OF PANDORA

Feeling blue? Get out and explore another planet!

Frontiers of Pandora should appeal to *Avatar* fans impatient for the next movie, because it's a completely standalone adventure set on a continent not seen in the movies so far. You play as a Na'vi orphan who's been raised by the human military, placed in suspended animation—then awakened years later by a group of Na'vi and human rebels. Your task is to travel the Western Frontier, organizing the Na'vi into a resistance force.

ON THE HUNT

■ The game also rewards you for killing animals cleanly and skillfully—a beast slain with an arrow will yield better meat than one shot to pieces with firearms. It makes you think about the world a different way!

SUPER DUPER FLY

■ The highlight of the game is flying on an ikran—and you can pull that awesome trick of jumping from a high place, then summoning your ikran to catch you.

FAST FACT

The game's developers have promised *Frontiers of Pandora* is fully part of the *Avatar* canon. "There is already some talk about maybe using some of the stuff that we did in the upcoming movies," creative director Magnus Jansén has said.

FRUIT TWIST

■ *Avatar* is all about respecting and being in tune with the environment, and a lot of attention has been paid to how you interact with it. When you harvest plants you need to twist them away, rather than just hitting a button or walking over them.

ENDGAME

■ Combat is pretty straightforward, but don't be fooled—the combat difficulty level really rises toward the end, and is geared more toward large waves of enemies than big bosses, so you'll really need those skills!

LIGHTSABER MASTERY IN STAR WARS JEDI: SURVIVOR

Struggling with the blade? Look on the light side!

The *Star Wars Jedi* games have brought balance back to the Force. Before they came along, *Star Wars* games were dominated by the military-style *Battlefront* series, which are cool but don't really capture the heroic adventure of the movies. *Star Wars Jedi: Survivor* hits the spot even better than *Fallen Order*, the first in the series, did. Best of all, it really gets inside what it's like to be a Jedi, with five different lightsaber stances!

1

Let's stance

You start the game with access to the Single Blade and Double Blade stances, both of which appeared in *Fallen Order*. The Dual Wield stance is unlocked after Coruscant, and enables Ahsoka-style combat with two lightsabers. Blaster stance, unlocked on Jedha, equips you with a blaster alongside your lightsaber. Crossguard uses a Kylo Ren–style lightsaber with smaller blades, and is unlocked at Shattered Moon.

2

Skill issue

Early on, it's worth trading two skill points to learn Aerial Assault for the Single Blade stance, but the best skills on each tree usually involve throwing the lightsaber: on Double Blade this is Controlled Throw (which lets you throw the lightsaber but also move it around); on Dual Wield it's Dancing Blades (both lightsabers bounce between opponents!); and on Crossguard, it's Rolling Thunder. Quick Draw is the handiest Blaster skill.

FAST FACT

You can change the color of your lightsaber at the workshop after playing through the introductory mission. Blue and green are the traditional Jedi colors, but seven others are available.

One-on-one

■ When confronting tough opponents, Blaster stance may be the best option because it allows you to keep your distance—though you'll need patience as your lightsaber attacks will be less powerful. Dual Wield, though effective at close range, leaves you super vulnerable. Crossguard offers good defense and the strongest attacks in the game, but makes you slower and more predictable. Double Blade is the way to go if you're getting swarmed by lots of enemies at once.

3

4

Secondary school

■ Don't forget, you can equip a secondary stance! If you're not sure of the situation, the versatile Single Blade is a good choice, but it's better to equip a secondary stance that complements the primary. For instance, with Double Blade, being able to switch to Dual Wield will let you make focused close-range attacks. If Dual Wield is your primary, give yourself ranged options by equipping Blaster stance.

Keeping it light

■ All this leaves you with a choice: constantly switch between stances or focus on getting absolutely cracked at one? Most players will benefit from the latter approach, especially as fully unlocking one skill tree will make you more powerful than unlocking a bit of them all. If you feel confident, you can start working on another stance—but you don't have to learn them all.

5

SUPER MARIO BROS. WONDER

A RETURN TO CLASSIC SIDE-SCROLLING *MARIO* ACTION!

Nintendo went back to basics with *Super Mario Bros. Wonder*, the first side-scrolling *Mario* game since *New Super Mario Bros. U* in 2012. In this adventure, Bowser seizes the reality-warping Wonder Flower and uses it to turn himself into a flying fortress—and Mario and co. must find the six Royal Seeds that will give them access to Castle Bowser . . .

Nintendo rarely misses with a *Mario* game, but *Wonder* is something special—it ranks alongside 2D classics such as *Super Mario World* and adds new mechanics like a drill hat, a bubble attack, and the ability to turn into an elephant. A four-player co-op mode and a clever online angle makes this a truly fresh spin on a classic!

QUICK TIPS

SPITTING ROOM

■ Yoshi has the Flutter Jump ability, which means he can reach high places more easily, and you can also grab with his tongue and spit. However, the Yoshis and Nabbit can't use transforming power-ups.

BLOCK AND REPORT

■ The other characters play the same, but each has their own character blocks, which are invisible when playing as a different character. These can still be activated in the same way as normal *Mario* invisible blocks, by hitting them from below.

TAKE IT EASY

■ You can choose from twelve characters. If you want an easier time, play as one of the four colored Yoshis or Nabbit. These characters don't take damage from enemies or hazards, though you can still die by falling off the screen.

BONUS TIME

The heart of any *Mario* game is its power-ups and collectibles. Mushrooms and Fire Flowers are there, of course, but *Wonder* adds a huge array of new items and ways to find them.

THE ELEPHANT IN THE ROOM

Collecting an Elephant Fruit triggers elephant form! Your character gains extra strength and can break blocks from the side—but a less obvious, and very handy, ability is that you can dash across gaps of two blocks.

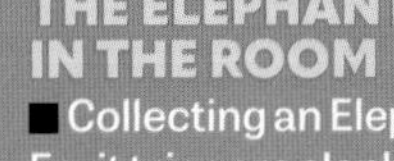

SPECIAL BADGES

The badges you collect can be equipped for additional effects. The most useful badge is actually the first one you obtain, Parachute Cap, but Grappling Vine and Coin Magnet are also very handy. Jump-boost badges will help you reach the top of flagpoles.

C'MON, BOUNCE

If you can keep a sequence of bounces going, whether it's off enemies or other objects, you'll see the words *Good*, *Great*, *Super*, *Fantastic*, *Excellent*, *Incredible*, and *Wonderful*—and then you'll start to get 1-Ups!

PURPLE PATCHES

Wonder has its own currency of purple Flower Coins, which can be spent in Poplin Shops. Almost every level has three ten-flower coins to find. If you are repeating a level and collect one again, it's only worth three.

LIKE THIS? TRY THIS:

SPELUNKY 2

Maybe you want some 2D platforming action but don't have a Switch—or maybe you've completed *Wonder* and want something more challenging. *Spelunky 2* invites you to explore some randomly generated caves and is pretty genius.

A WORLD OF WONDER

Here's some tips for getting 100-percent completion on *Super Mario Bros. Wonder*...

A good *Mario* player can speedrun the game in about ten hours—but as always, there's a lot more to find if you take the time to look. Don't miss out! There's no real reward—getting 100-percent completion doesn't unlock anything special—but half the fun of a *Mario* game lies in these hidden elements. You can always go back and explore levels you've already completed and unlike most *Mario* platformers there's no time limit, leaving you free to check every corner of the game.

1 We'll level with you

The game's map in *Wonder* is like a jazzed-up version of the one from *Super Mario World*. You start off on Pipe-Rock Plateau. Each level has a difficulty rating, so you know what you're in for, and some are optional, such as the Break Time! and Badge Challenge levels. There are also the Search Party levels, which—unusually for a 2D *Mario* game—are not linear. These have five Wonder Tokens to locate.

2 Seed capital

The game features 225 Wonder Seeds. Most levels have two: one when you complete the level, and another that can be found after activating the Wonder Effect for that level. A third may be found if the level has a secret exit. Some levels have only one Wonder Seed, such as the Search Party and Poplin House levels.

Pipe dreams

Each level's Wonder Effect changes the gameplay and transforms the whole level. For example, pipes may become Inchworm Pipes, which wriggle along and enable you to cross dangerous areas and reach higher places. In the Condarts Away! course, your character walks on the background walls when the Wonder Effect is triggered. On other levels, time may speed up or slow down. Any Wonder Effect ends after you locate the Wonder Seed.

3

4

Wonder visions

Some effects transform your character—in Where the Rrrumbas Rule, you turn into a spike ball, so you can damage enemies and break some materials. Some Wonder Effects are helpful, but some make the level more dangerous—for instance, on Fluff-Puff Peaks Flying Battleship you'll be targeted by a Bowser cannon. You'll want to find the Wonder Seed to make it stop!

FAST FACT

Amazingly, *Super Mario Bros. Wonder* is the fastest-selling *Super Mario* game ever, with sales of 4.3 million copies in its first two weeks. The original *Super Mario Bros.* has sold 58 million copies in almost forty years!

5

Keep your power

Sometimes in *Mario* games you find a power-up at the wrong time—you need it later, but you don't want it to wipe out the one you already have. *Wonder* lets you keep a power-up in reserve and choose when to use it by pressing A. This can make a huge difference in some stages, so think ahead when storing and using your power-ups!

Stand up for yourself

Some Wonder Effects, like the Bulrush Express, have a time limit and you must find the Wonder Seed before it ends. As well as finding seeds, you need to collect every Standee and badge, find all 306 purple ten-coins, and hit the top of each flagpole! Most shops sell you a random Standee for ten coins, but at the Special World shop you can choose your Standee for thirty coins.

FORTNITE AND ITS LASTING LEGACY

How going back helped *Fortnite* go forward!

During the first chapter of *Fortnite: Battle Royale*, the game was everywhere—everyone talked about it and the shops were full of *Fortnite* posters and T-shirts. While it may not be as fashionable these days, it's settled in to become part of the gaming landscape. Most importantly for a battle royale game, the lobbies are always busy, meaning players are never short of finding others for a match. But many players still have fond memories of the version they played during the *Fortnite*-mania of 2018 and 2019.

In November 2023, Epic launched a mini stopgap season between the fourth and fifth chapters—Season OG—which brought back the map and gameplay of the first chapter. Players old and new rushed back to the game, resulting in the highest-ever number of players jumping into *Fortnite*. Over 44.7 million players notched up over 102 million hours of play, with a peak of more than 6.1 million playing at once. Not surprisingly, once Season OG was over, Epic faced calls to bring it back—and it worked well as promo for the fifth chapter, too, with huge lines to get in the day it went live!

We thought OG was a good excuse to look back at how *Fortnite* changed gaming forever . . .

THE FREE-TO-PLAY MODEL

There had been many free-to-play games before *Fortnite*, in particular MMORPGs—but these were mostly limited to computers and mobile devices. *Fortnite* brought in a new era of cross-platform free-to-play games, and showed there was big money in it. With any battle royale game it's essential to have enough players online for a match at any time, and that's why making *Fortnite* free was the way to go. Epic Games has worked the same trick with *Fall Guys* and *Rocket League*, and the likes of *Genshin Impact* have had huge success with it.

THE BATTLE PASS

It's wild to think battle passes weren't really a thing before *Fortnite*. This simple system of paying up front and then earning rewards through play was introduced way back in season two, and still offers excellent value compared with buying items from the shop. Importantly, it keeps players coming back regularly, keeping the lobbies busy. So many games now use this system, especially in the free-to-play world—and it's great that *Fortnite*'s Battle Pass still offers more than enough V-Bucks to pay for the next one.

THE LORE

A game where everyone kills each other until only one is left alive shouldn't really work as an ongoing story. But *Fortnite* found a way, with the island trapped in a time loop where characters keep on coming back. The game's twisted lore has become a big part of its appeal!

THE COMPETITION

A wave of online battle royale games have emerged since *Fortnite* hit big with the format—most notably *Apex Legends*, which came out in 2019 when *Fortnite* was still in its first chapter. Some players rate *AL* above *Fortnite*, but there's no doubt the competition has pushed both games to come up with great new ideas (it was *AL* that invented the ping system). Strange to think *Fortnite: Battle Royale* began as a spin-off from a co-op tower defense game...

COMEBACK KINGS

■ Fortnite is always changing and introducing new things to keep players hooked—but that also means taking things out to make space. OG is a great blast from the past, letting you revisit Tilted Towers and remember what life was like before swimming was a thing. But every seasoned *Fortnite* player has something they miss that's been taken out of the game, and wish would make a comeback. Here are some of ours . . .

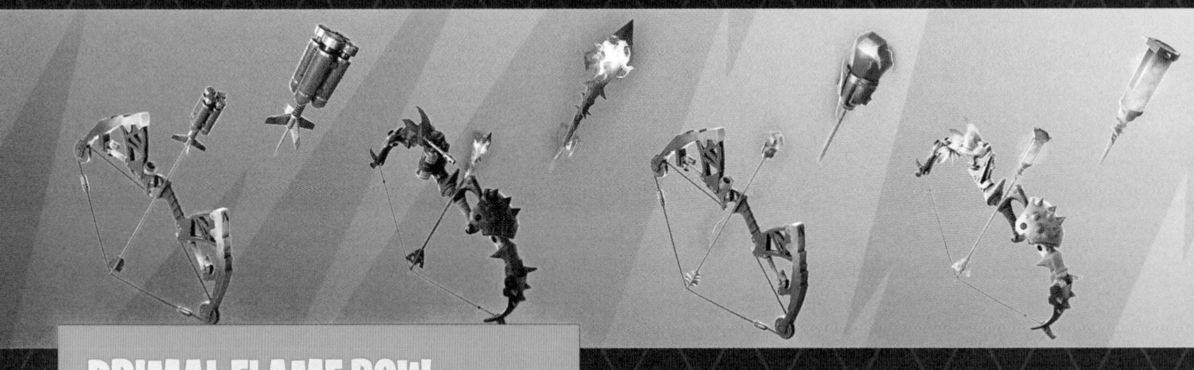

PRIMAL FLAME BOW

■ Introduced in Chapter 2 Season 6, this was great against those smug opponents in the endgame who keep building and building and building. Burn their tower from the bottom and watch it collapse! Also very effective against campers, opponents picking up dropped loot, and anyone taking cover to heal up, it's like having explosives and a ranged weapon all in one!

FLYING SAUCER

■ We really liked the choppers, but this vehicle from Chapter 2 Season 7 was even better because it had a tractor beam. This was fun for picking opponents up and dropping them—especially if they were in a car—but you could also hold a squadmate in it and lower them to open fire.

THE DAILY BUGLE

■ Peter Parker's workplace turned up in the middle of a dormant volcano, for some reason, at the start of Chapter 3. Its height made it a great landing spot, with lots of loot to be had as you worked your way down. And when it was in the game at the same time as tanks, you could ram the bottom floor away and watch the whole thing collapse! So yeah, while we're at it—bring back tanks.

KLOMBOS

■ These dinosaur-like beasts came in at the start of Chapter 3. Attacking them was pointless, as it just made them angry—instead you could feed them Klomberries in exchange for items, and even feed them an Exotic item to get a Legendary in return! And if you stood over their blowhole you could get propelled in the air and redeploy your glider. Easily the best animals ever in *Fortnite*!

PREDATOR

■ Not just the skin, which was pretty awesome, but the challenge you needed to complete to get it—hunt Predator down at Stealthy Stronghold. This was one of the best sub-games *Fortnite* has ever done!

FAST FACT

According to stats gathered by Fortnite.GG, the most-used *Fortnite* skin of all time is Aura, while the most popular skin from another franchise is *Tomb Raider*'s Lara Croft. Of the top 100 skins, 88 are female!

LEGO FORTNITE

The world of *Fortnite* is building!

At the end of 2023, *Fortnite* dropped its biggest new mode in years—*LEGO Fortnite*. Far more than just a LEGO-ized version of the existing game modes, *LEGO Fortnite* is a whole other thing—it's described as a "survival crafting" game, and yes, it's a lot like *Minecraft*. But there's also a community element that's more like *Stardew Valley*—other *Fortnite* NPCs rock up to your village as you build it, and they'll assist you if you give them the right facilities.

LEGO Fortnite has some advantages over *Minecraft*—it's free to play, it has a huge user base from *Fortnite*, and progress counts toward the current Battle Pass. So is it a true rival to the official Biggest Selling Game of All Time?

LEGO-IZED

■ When you open up your locker, it's impressive how many of *Fortnite*'s huge number of skins have been translated into LEGO versions. The characters from other franchises haven't been brought across, but almost every skin that's been created by Epic has a LEGO equivalent.

BLUEPRINT OR FREEBUILD?

■ One clever way the game mimics the experience of actually building LEGO is you are given blueprints for things where you have to follow instructions—but you also have the freedom to build your own things out of the pieces you've acquired!

LIVE AND LET DRY

■ Build workstations under cover, because if it rains you won't be able to use them. When you destroy them they drop the materials used to make them, so they won't be wasted if you need to break and remake them somewhere else.

CHASING BUTTERFLIES

■ Sometimes you'll see butterflies you can follow to find loot—but don't follow these until you've got a weapon, as they may lead you into dangerous territory. Spiders can be tackled with a punch, but wolves are too strong for that! Use your off-hand space for a shield, or a torch when it's dark.

A LITTLE HELP FROM YOUR FRIENDS

■ You can also invite NPCs to come with you when you go exploring—they'll help you to fight off threats, so you'll be able to focus more on getting materials. And you can strengthen yourself by crafting charms to increase your HP and cold resistance.

LEGO Fortnite is the first game from a "long-term partnership between Epic Games and the LEGO Group to develop fun and safe digital spaces for children and families"—so expect plenty more from them!

DETECTIVE PIKACHU RETURNS

THE WORLD'S SMALLEST, YELLOWEST DETECTIVE IS ON THE CASE AGAIN!

It's amazing to think the original *Detective Pikachu* came out so long ago, the Switch hadn't even been launched yet! This sequel picks up where the previous game left off, with Pikachu and Tim Goodman still searching for Tim's father, Harry. The sleuthing duo have become minor celebrities as a result of their activities, and soon get drawn into investigating a jewel robbery—which in turn opens out into a bigger, more interesting mystery.

The game's puzzles aren't too challenging and there's no game-over scenario. The fun of it is making the story unfold, and it improves over the first game in this aspect, with more excitement and intrigue. And who can fail to be charmed by the hard-bitten, coffee-chugging version of Pikachu these games offer up?

QUICK TIPS

LOCAL CONCERNS

■ Don't worry too much about the Local Concerns side quests. Do them if you want to complete the game and explore its world, but you won't earn anything that helps with the main story.

REFRESHER

■ Coming back after a break away from the game? It's a good idea to look back through the journal and refresh your memory about where you are in the case!

TAKE NOTE

■ The Quiz Professor will start to pop up after Chapter 1 and ask questions about Pokémon. If you see a professor, note where you saw them.

PUZZLING IT OUT

The process of detection is similar to the previous *Detective Pikachu*. Even if you've worked something out based on some of the evidence, collecting all the evidence is essential—you can't move forward with the case until you do!

LOG EVIDENCE

When looking around locations, click on every piece of evidence, not just things that need a closer look like documents and recordings. It all needs to be logged so make sure you don't miss anything!

BEGIN DEDUCING

The original game was on the 3DS, which used its second screen for Tim's journal. The Switch lacks that feature, so be sure to check the journal regularly.

HIGH AND LOW

Be sure to track down every clue and talk to every character at each location. Otherwise you'll have to go back for another look.

HERE TO HELP

At various points Pikachu can call on other Pokémon to help with the investigation, such as a Growlithe who can track down scents or a Luxray who can see through walls.

FAST FACT

This game ties off the Harry Goodman storyline, which the *Detective Pikachu* movie already did its own version of. So what will the sequel to the movie be about? We'll have to wait and see!

LIKE THIS? TRY THIS:

TANGLE TOWER

If you want a detective game that offers more of a challenge, *Tangle Tower* is a quirky, cool mystery in which Detective Grimoire and his assistant Sally attempt to unravel a thrilling mystery.

Song of Nunu: A League of Legends Story

A heartwarming snowbound adventure!

■ In recent years, *League of Legends* has really branched out from its long-running core online battle arena game with a range of single-player games set in the same world—and while *LoL* is only available on Windows and iOS, the spin-offs bring that world to consoles.

Following on from the turn-based RPG *Ruined King*, we've had a brawler in the form of *The Mageseeker*, a metroidvania called *Convergence*, and now *Song of Nunu*. This is a puzzle-platform adventure starring Nunu the Yotai and Willump the Yeti—a smart choice, as they feel right at home in this kind of game. It's the best *LoL* spin-off yet!

Added depth

■ Nunu and Willump have always been a team in *LoL*—their backstory is that Nunu went out to slay a monster and prove he was a hero, but ended up befriending the monster instead. It's also in their backstory that Nunu's mother is missing, and that's what drives this new adventure!

FAST FACT

The 2023 *League of Legends* finals took place in South Korea and was won by T1, who extended their record for the team with the most championships. T1's Lee "Faker" Sang-hyeok set his own record by becoming the first four-time champion.

Dream team

This is a single-player game, but you switch control between Nunu and Willump—and this is the fun of the environmental puzzles, working out who does what. It's a game with friendship at its heart, and the two of them talk to each other (well, Willump just makes Yeti sounds, but Nunu understands him).

Magic music

Nunu plays an instrument called the Svellsongur, and its music can affect the environment and characters. He also employs snowball-throwing skills to hit things that are out of reach. Meanwhile Willump can create ice and has climbing skills.

Avoiding trouble

LoL is all about combat, and this game seeks to offer something different—so while there is combat in it, there isn't that much. Nunu hops onto Willump's head during these sections and supports the attack by throwing snowballs.

Special guests

If you've never played *LoL* and know nothing about it, don't worry—*Song of Nunu* is a great standalone game that works perfectly for newcomers. But there are some nice cameo appearances from other Legends such as Braum and Lissandra.

CITIES: SKYLINES II

THE BIG-CITY SIMULATOR IS BACK AND IT'S EVEN BIGGER!

For decades the city-building genre was dominated by the *SimCity* franchise developed by Maxis. However, that franchise collapsed after a disastrous reboot in 2013 and Colossal Order stepped in with *Cities: Skylines*, which sold tons of copies because there are always people with "god complexes" wanting to build their own little world and run it how they like!

Now Colossal Order has followed up with a sequel, and instead of calling it *Cities: Something Else* they've gone with *Cities: Skylines II*. Unsurprisingly the premise hasn't changed: you're given a piece of undeveloped land and start building on it. A tiny village soon grows into a town, then a city. The sequel adds scale and new, more detailed management options. Now the size of your city is limited only by the technical specs of whatever you're playing it on!

QUICK TIPS

MAP TIME

■ Think carefully about your map choice. The buildable area changes from map to map, and the climate has an impact on how your citizens act and what they'll need.

WEATHER OR NOT

■ Cold or rainy weather will mean your citizens want indoor activities. Sunny or hot weather will increase the demand for outdoor attractions like parks. And colder climates mean they'll use more energy to heat their homes.

START SMALL

■ If you overbuild before your city develops, you may invest in the wrong things and waste money. Start by zoning 4x4 plots of low-density residential, so your citizens have affordable housing: large properties will have high rent.

THE URBAN SPRAWL

Cities: Skylines II divides your land into smaller tiles, allowing for more detailed building, but it also adds up to a much bigger space overall, covering 61 square miles (the original release covered 14 square miles).

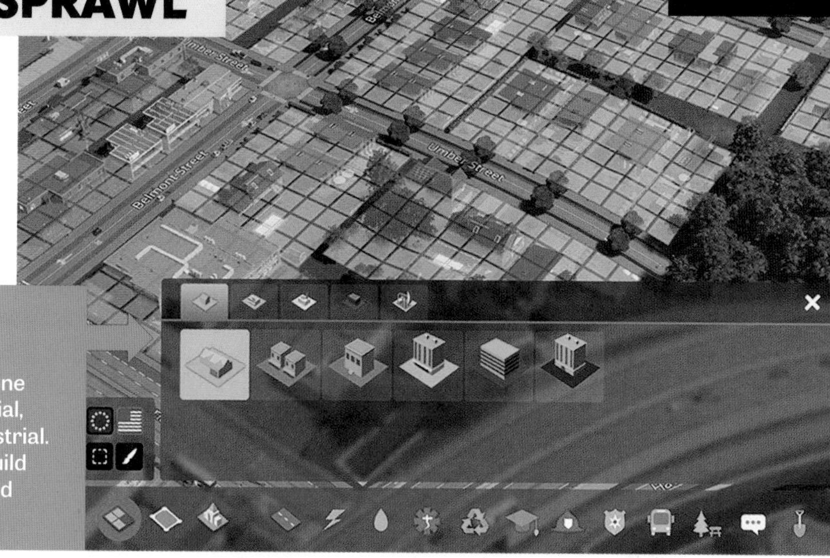

GET IN THE ZONE

Most of your buildings will come from zoning land into one of four categories—residential, commercial, office, and industrial. Once it's zoned, people will build on it. A mix of all four is needed for a successful city.

WHATEVER SUITS

Always pay attention to the Zone Suitability infoview, which pops up when zoning. This gives useful information about what kind of zone will work well, whether there's too much pollution for residential or the right type of customers for commercial.

BREATHING SPACE

Don't feel like you have to zone every inch of land. Leaving space between your buildings means that if there's a demand for something new, you won't have to upset people by re-zoning land that's been built on.

FAST FACT

The original *Cities: Skylines* supported user-created modification packs, and the new game does, too—but they're now available from Paradox Mods rather than Steam, so console gamers can get a hold of them as well as PC users.

CITY LIMITS

The larger playing area offers more scope to zone areas well outside the city. Citizens often dislike living near industrial zones due to the pollution, so you can create areas like this where they won't bother anyone.

MEET THEIR DEMANDS

City management is all about keeping track of the data—and *Cities: Skylines II* offers a lot of it. You need to keep track of demand among your citizens and respond to their needs. Don't be afraid to suspend the game if you need to look at problems and address them.

DAY-TO-DAY DATA

You can access loads of information about your citizens, meaning you can see which areas are growing and work out what people are likely to want. High-unemployment areas need more jobs, areas with young families need schools.

TOP OF THE TREE

Each Milestone unlocks a new Development Tree, where you can spend Development Points on new services and facilities, from waste water treatment to taxis. Eventually you can unlock everything—but in the meantime, prioritize what your city needs most.

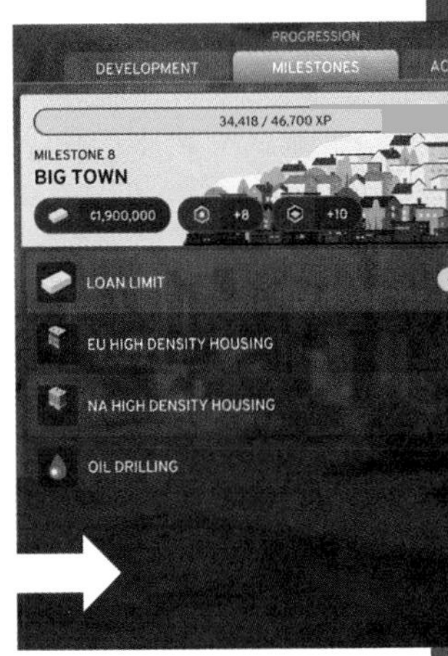

WHAT'S THAT GUY DOING?

In fact, you can access a pretty creepy level of data. You can literally see what this guy's name is, what he's doing, where he lives, and whether he's happy. And you can access the game world's own social media network and see what your citizens are talking about!

EXPAND ON THAT

The size of your population, the happiness of your citizens, and new additions to your city all contribute to your Expansion Points total. When you have enough points you can progress to the next Milestone, which brings new zone types, management options, and more!

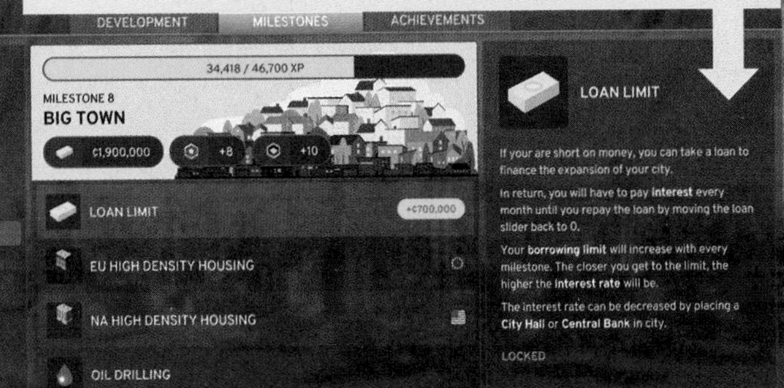

BUILDING A STYLE

You can set different architectural themes for your zones. The residential buildings on the left in this picture are North American style while the ones on the right are European style—you can mix or match them.

EYES ON THE ROAD

The tools for creating roads and railways have had an upgrade for this game, making laying down transport routes that much easier. And traffic AI is much smarter now, with your citizens making decisions based on more than just distance.

GO OFF-GRID

In older city-building games, you were forced to build roads on a rigid grid. Now you can shape them however you like, and they snap together neatly, too. (Some math skills may also be helpful to make sense of all the angle data.)

FIND AN ANGLE

But if you *want* your roads on a neat grid, there are also tools to make them run parallel, with perfect right angles and even spacing. You can build your roads to suit the city rather than building your city around the roads.

ON THE RIGHT LINES

You can also easily add features to roads after you've built them. If a street looks a bit stark and gray, you can add grass strips and trees—or you can add tramlines to give citizens extra transport options.

TRAIN THEM UP

Public transport is an essential investment. You'll get it at Milestone 4 and you should launch it as soon as possible, because complaints about traffic will quickly mount. Cargo transportation systems will also boost your economy.

LIKE THIS? TRY THIS:

ISLANDERS

If you want a city-building game that's not as heavy or detailed, for a more relaxed experience, *Islanders* is a more casual take on the genre, with simpler graphics and a points-based progress system.

CASSETTE BEASTS

A MUSICAL MONSTER-HUNTING ADVENTURE WITH A RETRO INDIE FLAVOR!

This is an RPG where you collect weird creatures of different types to use in a turn-based combat system... Yeah, it's a *Pokémon*-style game and it's not pretending it isn't. But it is one of the best *Pokémon*-style games ever made, and has loads of cute touches of its own—like how the creatures are captured using an old-school cassette.

Cassette Beasts is set on New Wirral, an island in a weird limbo, where the player wakes up stranded. The local settlement of Harbourtown is subject to attacks from the monsters who inhabit the island, and the residents take on monster forms to fight them off. But your aim is to find your way home, exploring the open world of New Wirral, solving puzzles, and finding dungeons. Keep that tape ready to roll!

QUICK TIPS

MAP TIME

■ The rumors you hear are useful in locating significant characters. You'll often find new rumors emerge after you've attained certain goals.

AY-CA-RUMBL-A

■ One of the handiest moves is Crumble. If opponents have elemental walls up, this will break through them in one blow and deal damage!

WEATHER OR NOT

■ As you unlock train stations, use them for fast travel thanks to Traffikrab. Some of them offer connections you might not expect, so explore them!

GET ON THE BEAT

■ The world of *Cassette Beasts* is so well designed. It uses a combination of 2D and 3D graphics, with a pixelated look and 1990s Nintendo-style chibi figures. It's like a Game Boy game suddenly lifted off the screen, and we love it.

OLDER AND WISER

■ The game has an array of quirky characters to meet, and while it's suitable for young gamers, it aims for a slightly older audience than *Pokémon*. *Pokémon* fans looking to move on to a new experience should check it out!

MAKING FRIENDS

■ As you complete quests for characters, you can make allies of them. They'll follow you around and support you in combat. You can also undertake further quests for them, which will increase your bond.

STAY IN RANGE

■ The Ranger HQ is an important location—you'll discover it early on, and while not all its services will be available at first, when you acquire fused materials you'll be able to swap them for upgrades.

IT'S GOT US BEAT

■ If you're going to make an adventure game with cassette-based combat, the music had better be good—and thankfully *Cassette Beasts* offers some stomping tunes. Proper songs with lyrics, too!

FAST FACT

Cassette Beasts' developer Bytten Studio is based in the UK, which explains the name of the game's location—the Wirral is a peninsula on Merseyside, near the city of Liverpool.

LIKE THIS? TRY THIS:

BUGSNAX

■ A weirder take on the "collect all the creatures" genre, this sees you exploring Snaktooth Island in search of the hybrid snack-bug creatures that inhabit it. The Muppet-like designs and the intriguing, surprisingly dark story create something really unique.

TALE OF THE TAPE

These tips will be music to your ears...

One cool aspect of *Cassette Beasts* is you don't catch monsters and keep them—instead, you take a recording of them on cassette during combat. Then, instead of sending monsters out to fight, you use the recording to *become* the monster for the duration of the fight.

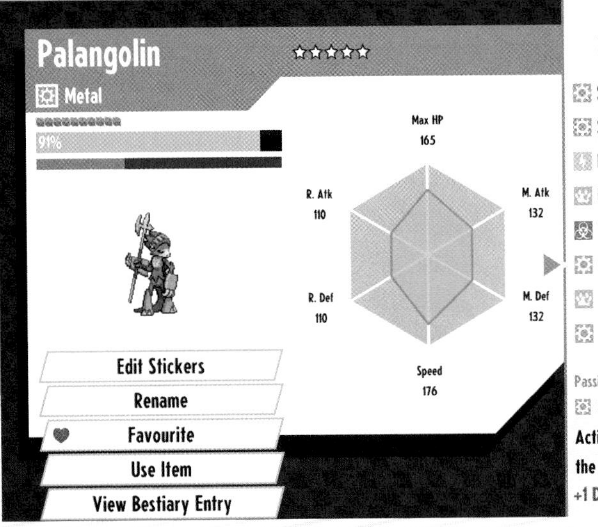

1

Stick it to 'em

Upgrades to your monsters take the form of stickers that you collect and stick to the tape. Different monsters have different numbers of sticker slots, but nearly all can be upgraded to a total of eight. There are also bonus sticker attributes, which may randomly be applied to a sticker when you receive it.

2

Use the fusion

There are 120 monsters in the game to collect—but here's the unique thing about *Cassette Beasts*: you can also fuse any two monsters during combat to create a new one. This expands the possibilities to an insane level. There are over *14,000* fusions you can discover!

FAST FACT

Tom Coxon, one of the two main creators on *Cassette Beasts*, also worked on *Stardew Valley*'s multiplayer mode, which was introduced in a 2018 update.

3

Turn down

■ Fusion is a powerful weapon, as it combines the moves and stats of both monsters. But there's a downside: because it involves two fighters becoming one, you only get one move per turn. It's best to save fusions for the tougher opponents, where you need more power.

4

How many?!

■ It kind of makes our heads hurt to think about that many creatures in one game. It's no surprise that, while some of them have been created by the developers, others use AI to merge the two monsters into one. But anyway, it means there's a lot to discover.

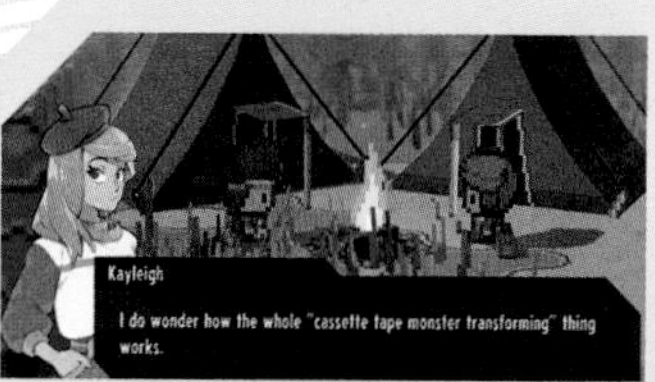

Sweet or spooky?

■ When talking to Kayleigh at the start of the game, you'll be asked to choose between "sweet" and "spooky." Sweet gives you Candevil as your starter, while spooky gives you Bansheep. Candevil has good ranged attacks and remasters into Malchemy (Poison-type) or Vendemon (Metal-type); Bansheep is better with melee attacks and remasters into Wooltergeist (Astral-type) or Zombleat (Earth-type).

5

Get it together

■ The game's co-op mode needs to be unlocked by completing the tutorial with Kayleigh. Once she's joined your party, another player can jump in and take control of whoever your current companion is—and jump out again.

TOP 10 HORROR AND SCARY GAMES

If jump scares are your thing, then leap on into this list of terror . . .

It's weird, but lots of people love to be scared—and video gaming has gotten better and better at providing those scares. It doesn't always have to be about gore or violence, either—the best scary games do it with weird visuals, unsettling noises, and sudden movements!

10 Stray

This is a cute game, right? You play as a stray cat in an underground sci-fi world without humans, accompanied by a drone, talking to robots and making your way to the surface. But along the way there are plenty of creepy moments, as you avoid the Zurks and the giant red eyes on the sewer walls. Be warned!

AVAILABLE ON:
PS5, PS4, Xbox Series S/X, Xbox One, PC, Mac

09 Goosebumps Dead of Night

This game follows on from the *Goosebumps* films, which were in turn based on the *Goosebumps* books—and Jack Black, who played writer R. L. Stine in the movies, also plays him in the games, which is cool. In this game he's been imprisoned inside his typewriter by the evil ventriloquist's dummy Slappy (also played by Black) and the player must come to the rescue. If you never found the books scary, you might be surprised by this game—it's got a vibe!

AVAILABLE ON: Nintendo Switch, PS4, Xbox One, PC

08 What Remains of Edith Finch

■ This amazing story-driven game sees you exploring a big old family house while the last surviving member of the family, Edith Finch, tells you how the others died. It's not difficult working your way through the game, but each story has its own minigame as well as a big dollop of tragedy. It's a short game, but its spookiness will stay with you!

AVAILABLE ON: Nintendo Switch, PS5, PS4, Xbox Series S/X, Xbox One, PC, iOS

06 Dredge

■ One of the most original horror games in years, *Dredge* takes you fishing in waters infested with sea monsters. It also transforms at night—while you can stay out on the water after dark, you'll start to panic, and that's when things get really weird...

AVAILABLE ON: Nintendo Switch, PS5, PS4, Xbox Series S/X, Xbox One, PC

07 Slender: The Arrival

■ Slender Man has become a pretty big deal in the horror world considering it started life as a meme, and *The Arrival* is one of the most genuinely scary games out there. You explore abandoned locations and avoid Slender, with only a flashlight to defend yourself. It's pretty short—but could you handle playing it for longer? It first came out in 2013, but has been remastered for current-gen consoles.

AVAILABLE ON: Nintendo Switch, PS5, PS4, Xbox Series S/X, Xbox One, PC

04 Little Nightmares

■ You play as Six, a nine-year-old girl trapped in a weird underwater base called The Maw. It's puzzle-based—you must try to make your way through the base and not get killed, including avoiding the attention of the disturbing figures that live in The Maw's rooms. A lot of it's based on stealth, which makes it extra tense. It's tricky, but it brings the horror so well! The sequels are also recommended.

AVAILABLE ON: Nintendo Switch, PS5, PS4, Xbox One, PC, Stadia, iOS, Android

05 Poppy Playtime

■ In the style of *Five Nights at Freddy's*, this is about cute kids' stuff turning deadly—in this case, giant cuddly toys that stalk an abandoned toy factory killing people. It's not as scare-heavy as some games—a lot of the time you're solving puzzles to progress through the factory—but when you do get chased by something terrifying, it's a real challenge to get away from it! The lore is very weird, but the old adverts and the creepy 1980s-style *Smiling Critters* cartoon are brilliantly done.

AVAILABLE ON: Nintendo Switch, PS5, PS4, PC, iOS, Android

03 Hello Neighbor

■ Like many great games, this is based on a simple idea: Your neighbor has a secret, so you have to break into his basement and find it without getting caught by him. What's clever is how the neighbor learns from what you do and will try to stop you getting in the same way. The story gets pretty bleak and strange toward the end!

AVAILABLE ON: Nintendo Switch, PS4, Xbox One, PC, iOS, Android, Stadia

02 Five Nights at Freddy's

■ *Five Nights at Freddy's* is such a huge deal now, it's weird to remember it started as a simple game where you have to check monitors and close the right doors at the right times. The scope of recent games like *Security Breach* and its excellent DLC *Ruin* is much bigger, but at the core of it all is a growing lore about someone so evil he can't be destroyed, who keeps haunting different pizza restaurants. And now it's produced a hit film, it seems destined to run and run.

AVAILABLE ON: PS5, PS4, Xbox Series S/X, Xbox One, PC, iOS, Android, Stadia, Oculus Quest

01 Subnautica

■ *Subnautica* looks like it might be one of those relaxing, soothing game experiences. It isn't. It's set on an ocean planet the player has crash-landed on. You make your way through its waters, searching for a wrecked ship, and some of the sights you see are awe-inspiring and beautiful… But a lot of the time you're trying to avoid being killed by terrifying sharklike beings. While most horror games trap you in a space, this one does the opposite—you're stranded in the open sea with no safe place to go. One of the scariest games we've played!

AVAILABLE ON: Nintendo Switch, PS5, PS4, Xbox Series S/X, Xbox One, PC, iOS

FAST FACT

There's also a sequel, *Subnautica: Below Zero*, set in a frozen biome on the same planet as the original, but with a new character investigating her sister's death.

FAE FARM

RELAX, GROW SOME CROPS, EXPLORE DUNGEONS, KILL MONSTERS.

It's strange to think ten years ago, farm sims weren't really a genre—there was just one game series, *Story of Seasons* (also known in English as *Harvest Moon* after the first game), that did that kind of thing. But then when *Stardew Valley* came along and was such a hit, other people have been inspired to do their own take on it.

The 2020s are seeing a rush of farm sims like *Immortal Life*, *Harvestella*, *Disney Dreamlight Valley*, *Coral Island*, *Rune Factory 5*, *Ooblets*, and now *Fae Farm*, on Switch and Windows. Like many of these games, Fae Farm has a combat element, but overall it's a low-stakes, low-conflict experience, offering the relaxed, escapist vibe farm sim fans are looking for.

QUICK TIPS

ANIMAL LOVER

■ Your magical farm animals are more low-maintenance than you might expect—you don't have to look after them constantly, so once they're producing you can focus elsewhere.

RAMPING UP

■ The game's world gets more interesting after Chapter 4, with new areas, new abilities, and new characters unlocked—so get to the bottom of Saltwater Mines as fast as you can!

WARM UP

■ Be sure to upgrade your mining skills and pickax when you can, because you'll get more profit from your mining activities that way—and this is the best way to earn money.

AROUND AZORIA

The game begins with you being shipwrecked on an island called Azoria that's home to a farming community. After being rescued by the mayor you're given a farm to develop and can settle in.

GET IT DUNGEON

There are three dungeons in Azoria, each with multiple levels. Exploring these and grabbing their resources are important to your progress. Magic potions can offer protection or enable you to pass unseen.

SAFE AT HOME

There are monsters called Jumbles, who have been created by wild magic, and other hazards on the island—but death isn't really a thing here. Instead of being killed you'll end up back in town.

KEEP COZY

The effects of customizing your home is more than just cosmetic. Making new furniture boosts your cozy rating, which in turn raises your maximum health, energy, and mana.

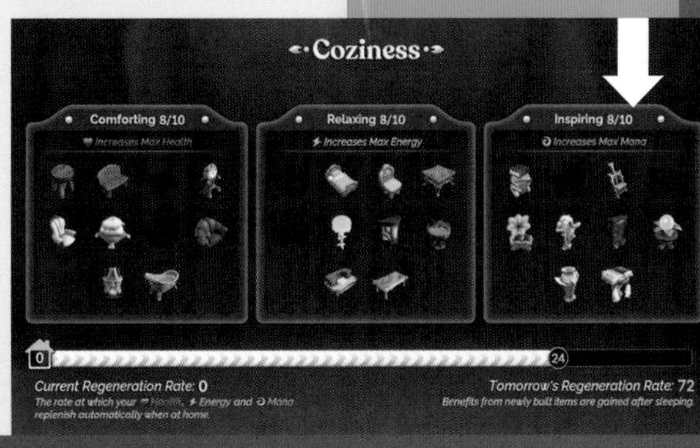

STAY OUT LATE

It's generally a less-stressful experience than most farm sims. You don't have to rush home at the end of the day, and movement and navigation have been well designed so you're less likely to get frustrated.

LIKE THIS? TRY THIS:

HARVESTELLA

A beautiful anime-style farm sim with a touch of *Final Fantasy* about it, this has more of an RPG element compared to other farm games: it opens during Quietus, the season of death that makes crops wither.

GETTING STARTED ON FAE FARM

Set yourself on the right path with these tips.

Fae Farm is a much bigger game than it might look at first glance. There's a lot to explore, and you'll make faster progress if you start well—so here are five important things to bear in mind as you set out on life in Azoria.

1

Break fast

■ Your priority early on should be to get the fast travel mechanic working. Unlock and craft the Seal Crafting Station and find out what seals you need to make to activate the pedestals, including the one at your home ranch. This will save so much time when you need to gather items.

FAST FACT

Phoenix Labs' previous game was the free-to-play MMO action RPG *Dauntless*, released via Epic Games in 2019 and expanded across all major platforms.

2

Seal the deal

■ Seals can also be used in dungeons. Place them on each level in turn and you'll be able to fast travel between the floors. This will enable you to take each dungeon in stages, rather than trying to complete it in one go. So focus on getting the materials to make each Seal.

3 Return trips

Prepare well for dungeons: magic potions and meals with special benefits will help you a lot. Also, this isn't one of those games where you complete a dungeon and then it's done and you never have to think about it again: You'll need to go back and gather items later in the game.

4 Keep good stocks

Early on you'll acquire plenty of items you don't immediately need. However, you will need them later—so don't cash them all in and make money for upgrades. We suggest not letting your stock of anything go below ten.

Fae fishing

Like roughly 57 percent of all games these days, *Fae Farm* includes fishing—but it's a little more advanced than just casting your line into the water and reeling in when it jerks. You need to spot the fish and work out their movement patterns, then cast your lure so it lands where the fish will see it. It helps if you jiggle the lure a few times. You can also eat meals that temporarily boost your fishing skills!

5 Master crafters

Most upgrades to tools are handled by Cinder, who works near the Docks. However, nets are upgraded by Mel in West Town, while Eddy in Stay-A-While Bay deals with fishing rods. You may have missed this info if you skipped a lot of the dialogue!

DISNEY ILLUSION ISLAND

YOU WON'T BELIEVE YOUR EYES!

Back in 1990, no one had done anything remotely cool with Mickey Mouse in a long time. Then Sega made *Castle of Illusion Starring Mickey Mouse* for the Mega Drive, a console that desperately needed its own *Mario*—and did an excellent job of it. *Castle of Illusion* got rave reviews and even gamers who weren't Disney fans found themselves drawn into its sinister cartoon world.

Three sequels followed, and a remaster appeared in 2013, but the last new game in the series was 1995's *Legend of Illusion*—until *Disney Illusion Island*, released on the Switch. With Mario going back to 2D for *Super Mario Bros. Wonder*, this feels like a perfect time to revisit the classic side-scrolling style of *Castle of Illusion*.

QUICK TIPS

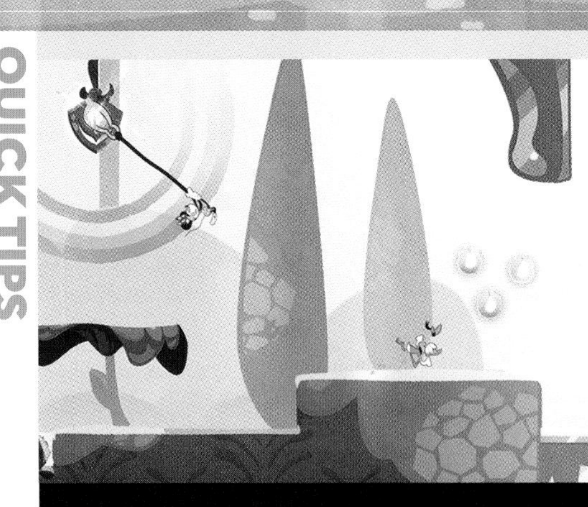

EAGLE EYES

■ Look out for walls with chips taken out of them. This always means the wall can be walked through to access a secret area.

HEALTH PLAN

■ When you pass a mailbox and autosave, you can leave the game and return as a different character with full health.

SWING LOW

■ When you grapple and swing along upside-down rainbows, you can travel back the other way if you keep holding the Y button—it's easier than swinging up and coming back.

A NICE DAY OUT GONE WRONG

Our heroes are planning a picnic on an island called Monoth, but soon learn bandits have stolen the three Tomes of Knowledge from the library there and are tasked with finding them. Don't you hate it when that happens?

FRIENDS WITH A LOT IN COMMON

You have a choice between Mickey, Minnie, Donald, and Goofy, but don't waste too much time pondering which one to pick—they all play exactly the same, though their animations are different.

LOOKING SHARP

Illusion Island scores an immediate win with its art style, which really freshens up these familiar characters. They lean toward cartoony rather than cutesy, and have a classic hand-drawn feel with a modern twist.

LITTLE HELP HERE?

The game also has a great co-op mode unlike some co-op platformers where you're simply playing in the same space. You can drop ropes to help each other to high ledges and even teleport each other clear of trouble.

HUG IT OUT

There's another cute aspect of the co-op mode—if one party member is low on hearts, another member can give them a hug and restore a heart to their health bar. Aww.

FAST FACT

The 2013 *Castle of Illusion* remake is still available on Steam. The original game was included on the Mega Drive Mini, if you can find one . . .

LIKE THIS? TRY THIS:

RAYMAN LEGENDS

The fifth game in the *Rayman* series was a slow seller but has become recognized as a classic of the platform genre, and was ported to the Switch, Xbox One, and PS4 so you can still access it today.

WILD HEARTS

BE A MYSTERIOUS STRANGER TRAVELING INTO DANGER!

Wild Hearts offers a real challenge to Capcom's all-conquering *Monster Hunter* series. It's set in a fantasy version of feudal Japan. An unnamed hunter arrives in the land of Azuma and seeks to take down Kemono, the huge monsters that plague the town of Minato.

Anyone who's a keen fan of the *Monster Hunter* series and is impatiently waiting for the next game will find a lot to like here. At the same time, it's a little simpler than those games and has a back-to-basics feel—so if you've never played any monster-hunting games before and want to get into it, this is a great place to start.

QUICK TIPS

STRIKE A POSE

Try setting your Karakuri Stance to Hold instead of Toggle. You may find this makes using Karakuri in combat easier, as you'll switch straight back into fighting and moving when you release the button.

HUNTER GATHERER

After a fight, the loot from a slain Kemono automatically becomes yours—but any parts chopped off during battle don't, so quickly collect them before you return to camp.

BOOK SMART

Do your research! The in-game Cyclopedia has information on any Kemono you've encountered, so read up on them and learn their strengths and weaknesses, then plan your attack accordingly.

JOIN THE FIGHT

Wild Hearts has a story that unfolds over four chapters and four main locations—Harugasumi Way, Natsukodachi Isle, Akikure Canyon, and Fuyufusagi Fort. (There's also Minato and Sacred Mountain.) And there are monsters *everywhere*.

TOUGHEN UP

The Kemono look great and are satisfying to fight, though there isn't a huge amount of variety in them. You'll probably find them tough to beat at first, and will need to take on some side quests to level up.

LOOKS LIKE RAIN

There are eight different weapon tiers including blades, bows, staffs, hammers, cannons, and this umbrella-looking thing, which is actually a Bladed Wagasa. You can use it to attack and also to parry enemy attacks.

OBEY THE CLAW

Unlike some games where the differences between weapons are pretty small, the ones in *Wild Hearts* play very differently. The Claw Blade is a favorite, allowing you to make flurry attacks, though it's tricky to learn.

KNOW YOUR WAY AROUND

Combat skills are important, but you also need to analyze the maps and deploy your resources to their best advantage. Each region is kind of like a puzzle, and the art of Karakuri is the solution . . .

FAST FACT

The design team aimed for the Kemono to be as menacing and deadly as possible, not just to make the game exciting and challenging, but also so you don't have to feel bad about killing them.

LIKE THIS? TRY THIS:

MONSTER HUNTER RISE

Obvious, but true—if you like *Wild Hearts* and have never played a *Monster Hunter* game, you really should! In *Rise* you're accompanied by a Palamute, which is basically a dog and is a blast to play.

WILD HEARTS KARAKURI GUIDE

We'll help you master this awesome ancient technology!

The most distinctive part of *Wild Hearts* is its system of Karakuri devices. Some of these are designed to be used in combat, others are deployed to help you outside combat. There are three types—Basic, Fusion (combinations of Basic Karakuri), and Dragon. There's an unlockable skill tree for these—don't forget to use your Kemono Orbs to unlock new ones. Here are some of the best and how to use them.

1

The four areas of the game world are based on the four seasons: Harugasumi Way is spring, Natsukodachi Isle is summer, Akikure Canyon is fall, and Fuyufusagi Fort is winter.

Spring

This Basic Karakuri does exactly what you'd expect—it sends you flying into the air when you stand on it. This can be a great way to escape from some Kemono who are simply too large and fast to dodge when they charge—be ready with a Spring and face the way you want to jump.

2

Bulwark

This is a Fusion Karakuri made from six Crates, combined into a 2x3 cuboid. Bulwarks and Crates can be placed in combat to block attacks as well as to launch your own attacks: the Bulwark, as you would expect, is a stronger structure and can deflect some pretty powerful Kemono assaults.

3

Managing your energy

■ Dragon Pits don't have unlimited energy—the more Karakuri you place, the more energy they drain off. So if you don't need a particular Karakuri any more, consider removing it and freeing up energy for new ones. There are five different types of energy—Earth, Wind, Fire, Water, and Wood—so keep an eye on which types your Karakuri are using.

4

Hunting Towers

■ These are the best Karakuri in the game, as they track Kemono—though like all Dragon Karakuri they must be powered by a nearby Dragon Pit. Look at your map and try to find places to deploy as few Hunting Towers as possible to cover the entire region—then you'll be able to follow all Kemono activity there.

New look

■ Not happy with your avatar's appearance? Regretting that beard? Or maybe you're stuck with a goofy name. You'll need to unlock the Looking Glass Karakuri, which is quite a way down the skill tree—but when you craft one, you'll be able to change your appearance and name for free. Build it in Minato, because it's a real drain on Dragon Pits!

5

Hunter's Tent

■ This Dragon Karakuri creates a respawn point and can be used for fast travel, so it's worth spreading some around. You may not be able to afford to place many, so look out for the secret camping spot in each region where tents can be pitched for 10 percent of the usual price!

STAR WARS OUTLAWS

Become a scoundrel in a galaxy far, far away!

Outlaws is the first-ever open-world *Star Wars* game. In fact it's not just open-world—it's open-*worlds*. The planets you can explore are a combination of ones seen in the films, like Kijimi and Tatooine; ones from the expanded universe, like Akiva; and new planets such as the moon of Toshara. It's a smart contrast to the honorable questing of *Star Wars Jedi: Survivor*—in this, you play as a cunning lowlife criminal...

OPEN UNDERWORLD

■ *Outlaws* is set between the events of *The Empire Strikes Back* and *Return of the Jedi*. It takes place in the galactic underworld, away from the conflict between the Empire and the Rebel Alliance.

ONE LAST BIG SCORE

■ You play as Kay Vess, who's planning an epic heist—and hoping to make a new start with the loot. It's very cool how she fits in with the late 1970s/early 1980s look of the original *Star Wars* films.

FAST FACT

You may recognize ND-5's voice—that's Dee Bradley Baker, who has played many roles in the animated *Star Wars* shows including all the clone troopers in *The Bad Batch*. He was also the voice of Waddles in *Gravity Falls*.

GETTING A BAD REP

■ The game operates on a faction reputation system, which means the way you act has a lasting effect. If you steal from people, your reputation with them will go down; if you're friendly with them, your reputation may rise.

WHAT YOU WANT?

■ You may be declared "wanted by the Empire"—and then have to avoid being captured. If you can dodge them for long enough, they'll stop looking. You may be able to avoid becoming wanted at all by bribing the right people!

YOUR HOMIES

■ Kay's companions are Nix, a Merqaal, and ND-5, a BX-series droid who fought in the Clone Wars. Other characters who make an appearance include Jabba the Hutt, Salacious B. Crumb, and Han Solo—stuck in carbonite, as he was at the end of *The Empire Strikes Back*.

SUPER MARIO RPG

A FRESH LOOK FOR ONE OF MARIO'S WEIRDEST ADVENTURES!

Super Mario RPG: Legend of the Seven Stars originally came out on the SNES in 1996, and was a totally new type of *Mario* game, combining the characters and background of the *Mario* platform games with the more exploration-based style of games like *Final Fantasy*. In fact, while *Mario* games were usually made in-house by Nintendo, this one was developed by Square, the company behind *Final Fantasy*.

This bizarre and comical adventure was a big hit, and it's made a few comebacks on the Wii and Wii U virtual consoles and on the SNES Classic Edition. Now it's had a full remaster for the Switch with all-new graphics, but how does it stack up against more recent games like *Paper Mario*?

QUICK TIPS

HE'S A FUN GUY!

■ Unlike in the main-series *Mario* games, you can save special items for later—but you don't have to! There's plenty of stuff around. Visit Forest Maze if you need Mushrooms.

DO YOUR HOMEWORK

■ It's well worth reading the descriptions of each character's special attacks—there are ways to make them extra effective, and it's easier to read up on them instead of guessing!

MAKING MONEY

■ In the remake you can't sell any unique equipment you get a hold of, but you should definitely sell everything else when you have replaced it with something better.

IF IT'S NOT BROKEN, DON'T FIX IT

Under those new graphics, *Super Mario RPG* has hardly been changed. In fact, while the graphics are more detailed and movement is smoother, they haven't done anything too flashy with it.

FOLLOW THE SCRIPT

This means you get all the same dialogue from the original, which is a very good thing because this is one of the funniest *Mario* games ever made!

MINIGAME MADNESS

In places the game has a surprising *Mario Party* vibe, as it breaks out into minigames. You may find yourself trying to grab coins as you tumble down a waterfall…

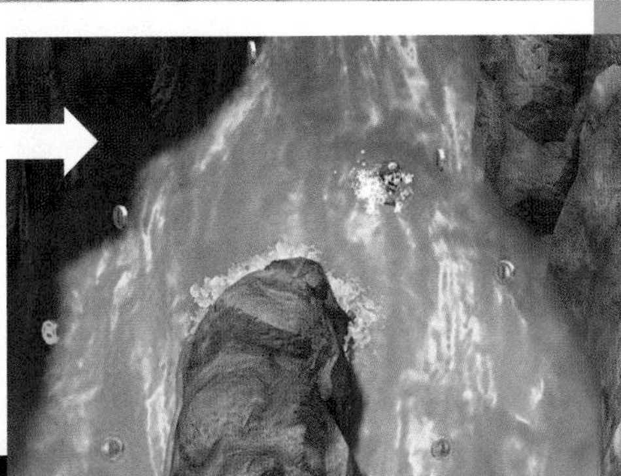

A TAD MUSICAL

…or hopping across musical tadpoles to create a tune. It's one of the weirdest and most creative *Mario* games, and everything that made the original great is still there!

LET'S GO AGAIN

And when you finish the game, this unlocks a new postgame mode. You can reexplore the world to get 100-percent completion, but there's also a mini-quest from the Frog Sage where you can stage tougher rematches with the bosses!

FAST FACT

The music from the original game has been rerecorded with live instruments by original composer Yoko Shimomura, and you can choose to have the new or the classic version when playing! After finishing the game you can listen to the music from the menu.

LIKE THIS? TRY THIS:

LINK'S AWAKENING

Another classic Nintendo RPG from the 1990s that's had the remaster treatment, this is the best classic *Zelda* action you can get on the Switch—a weird, magical adventure that sees Link shipwrecked on an island.

SUPER MARIO RPG TRIPLE MOVES GUIDE

Read on if you want to be a triple threat!

Super Mario RPG uses a turn-based combat system, and new elements have been added for the remaster. Triple Moves have been introduced—these can be used when you time your hits really well and fill up a gauge. Watch this gauge—these are powerful attacks, so use them when you can!

1

The right team for the job

■ Combat involves picking a team of three—once you've met enough characters, that is. Different characters have different skills, so Peach heals while Bowser is all about high-damage attacks. Your lineup also alters what Triple Move you can use, so think about what move you need before you start a battle!

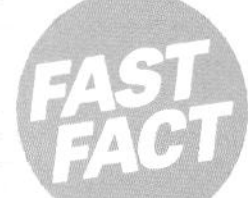

In Japan, the Mushroom Kingdom's princess was always called Peach—but in English-speaking countries she was renamed Princess Toadstool. *Super Mario RPG* was one of the last games to use Toadstool, and in the new version that's been changed to Peach.

2

Random Toad

■ You won't get the full roster until Peach joins you at level 9. When you only have two fighters available—either because you haven't found more yet, or because one of your party has been knocked out—that means you get Toad Assist, where Toad rocks up and randomly attacks or heals!

3

Shell company

With Mario, Peach, and Bowser you can use Starry Shell Spike—this is a high-damage attack that hits all enemies by launching an invincible Bowser. Mario, Mallow, and Geno give you Star Riders—this does focused damage to one spot, making this the ideal combo to take into boss battles.

4

Clowning around

Clown Car Barrage needs Mario, Mallow, and Bowser, and this launches a barrage of fire, ice, and electrical elemental attacks, plus a bomb. Playing with Mario, Bowser, and Geno provides Shooting Star Shot, where the full party gets a boost for three turns, and Geno unleashes randomly targeted attacks.

Keep a spare

There's a defensive move, Spare-Us-All, which is activated with Mario, Peach, and Geno—this will protect you from one attack, so time your use of this one carefully.

There's also a healing move, Healing Rainbow, which needs Mario, Mallow, and Peach, and will not only revive all your team, but also bring you back to full HP.

5

Ace team

Although there was never a direct sequel to *Super Mario RPG*, several of the team who developed that game went on to create the *Mario & Luigi* series of RPGs for Nintendo's handheld consoles.

THE BEST BATTLE ROYALE TIPS

Struggling to claim those sweet victories? We can help!

Battle royale games like *Fortnite*, *Apex Legends*, and *Overwatch 2* all have their own particular mechanics and rules, but most of the basics are the same: a large number of players drop into a space, pick up loot, and try to eliminate each other while the arena shrinks. We've compiled some tips you can apply to most—or all—these games to improve your chances of victory!

GO SOMEWHERE QUIET

In some battle royales you don't get a choice of where you start, but with the drop-ship approach of *Fortnite* and *Apex Legends*, many players either bail out straightaway or head for the thick of the action. If it's victory you want, stay on until the last moment and go somewhere quiet. Often you can load up at your leisure, and by the time you're ready to move on, half your opponents are out of the game. If you're at the edge of the map and there's no one else in your landing spot, then when the map starts to shrink, you can be pretty sure no one will sneak up behind you.

ZIGZAG

■ If there's any chance someone might be lining you up in the sights of their sniper rifle, be very wary of moving in a straight line! If someone is directly behind you, you're making their shot so much easier, so run in a zigzag pattern. Do the same thing when running to engage with enemies—in *Apex Legends* you can super glide while zigzagging, which makes you a really tricky target.

APEX LEGENDS

TAKE THE HIGH GROUND

■ Generally, in a straight fight the player with the higher ground is at an advantage. You can control the situation better because it's easier for you to drop down than for them to come up. Your sightlines are less likely to be blocked, and it's easier to get a headshot from above than from below. You should also bear this in mind when crouching—it can be a great way to avoid being seen and heard, but when a fight begins, straighten up at the earliest opportunity.

OVERWATCH 2

BE PATIENT

■ If you've got a safe spot inside a building, there's nothing wrong with staying there. Close all doors behind you, to make opponents less likely to suspect someone's inside, and make sure your weapons are loaded (this is an important general tip—constantly check they're loaded and be aware of any noise they make). If there are no buildings to hide in, try bushes—or vehicles. Opponents often fail to spot someone sitting in a car with its engine off!

FORTNITE

COMMUNICATE

When engaging with an enemy squad, your squad shouldn't each take on a different opponent. If you all focus your fire on one enemy and take them down, that's one enemy who's not firing back. The key to this is communication and sticking together. If you're all on the same page and the other squad isn't, you've got a much better chance of eliminating them. Even if you don't have a mic, or aren't able to type messages to your comrades, you can use ping to indicate targets.

OVERWATCH 2

ATTACK IN THE AFTERMATH

If you hear gunfire being exchanged, cautiously head toward it. Players in combat will probably be too focused on one another to notice you, and you can position yourself to take them on. Wait for one side to eliminate the other, then take on any survivors while they're healing or grabbing loot—they'll be weakened from the fight and should be easy pickings. And be aware of others doing the same thing to you!

APEX LEGENDS

CHECK OUT CHALLENGES AND QUESTS

A lot of players don't bother looking at the XP-earning tasks—but often they're very simple to do, especially if you're staying out of busy parts of the map. You can spend the early part of a match quest-grinding, then get involved toward the end. This doesn't just help you zoom up the levels—often it helps you learn new elements of the game, and practice skills you don't otherwise use!

FORTNITE

OTHER BATTLE ROYALE STYLES

Want a change of pace? Here are some different takes on the battle royale!

FALL GUYS

■ This combines obstacle races, playground-style games, survival challenges, and more. You and up to thirty-nine other players guide your little jellybean guys through these elimination rounds until you reach the final. The trickiest thing about this is the rounds are selected at random, so you can't practice them—which means the final round in particular is very hard to get good at unless you play a lot!

TETRIS 99

■ In the two-player version of classic *Tetris*, lines that vanished from one player's screen appeared on the other player's screen. *Tetris 99* does the same thing, but with one hundred players at once! Your strategy for where you send your lines is very important—you can target a particular player, strike back at someone who's targeting you, hit players who are close to elimination, go for those who've earned badges from good play, or just pick on someone at random!

FORZA HORIZON

■ After the release of *Forza Horizon 4*, a new battle royale game mode called the Eliminator was added, in which seventy-two players are put in the game world in a low-spec car. They can find better cars from car drops as they drive around the map, or they can win an opponent's car by beating them in a head-to-head race. Losers in such races are eliminated and so are players who drive out of the shrinking safe zone. A final race between survivors decides the winner. It proved so popular, *Forza Horizon 5* brought in the mode from the start!

SUPER ANIMAL ROYALE

■ OK, this one is based on shooting at each other with guns, but it's cuter and wackier than most battle royale games, with sixty-four cartoon animals fighting one another to find a winner. What other game lets you run over opponents in a hamster ball?

STREET FIGHTER 6

WE'VE STILL GOT LOVE FOR THE STREETS!

The *Street Fighter* series has been the biggest name in fighting games since *Street Fighter II* was a megahit in arcades and on consoles in the 1990s. Some fans were a little disappointed by the fifth game in the series, but *Street Fighter 6* more than makes up for it—it's the biggest *Street Fighter* game yet.

The heart of the game is still one-on-one combat between anime-ish characters from around the world, with different fighting styles and wild special moves, who seem to have plenty of money to fly from country to country just to beat each other up. But, this time, Capcom has added extra depth and features that make this much more than a next-gen upgrade—it's possibly the best *Street Fighter* game ever!

QUICK TIPS

BOREDOM BUSTER!

■ Blocking may seem boring compared with flashy attacks, but you can't get truly good at the game until you learn to do it well!

TRAIN TO GAIN

■ Training Mode is great for learning new characters and moves before trying them out in a match. Don't worry about combos at first—focus on getting control of the arena.

ROLE PLAY

■ Try out all the characters—you may be surprised by which ones work for you, and even if they don't, you'll know them better for when you come up against them.

FIGHTING AROUND THE WORLD

Street Fighter has come a long way from the days when it was just one fight after another. *Street Fighter 6* has a lot to explore, and the fighters have a bigger moveset than ever.

DRIVE YOUR POINT HOME

The major new fighting addition is Drive, a charged meter you can use for five different attacks: Impact, Parry, Reversal, Rush, and Overdrive. You get six bars of Drive, and matches can get tough if you run out!

STORYTELLER

World Tour is the game's story mode. This could easily have been an afterthought, but it's like a whole extra game. In this you create your own fighter and level them up.

RELAX

The online Battle Hub has had more effort put into it than your average lobby—there are even arcade cabinets where you can play classic games including *Street Fighter II*!

PLOTTING

Story mode is good if you're new to *Street Fighter*, because it has training side quests that will teach you the basics. It's also fun to fight random people on the street.

FAST FACT

In the original *Street Fighter*, which came out in 1987, players could only choose between Ryu and Ken, and all the characters came from Japan, China, the United States, or England.

LIKE THIS? TRY THIS:

MARVEL VS CAPCOM: INFINITE

This fighting game also features *Street Fighter*'s Ryu and Chun-Li alongside characters from other Capcom titles like *Monster Hunter* and *Mega Man*, and pits them against characters from the Marvel universe! You could also check out *Dragon Ball FighterZ*.

STREET FIGHTER 6: BEST CHARACTERS AND FIGHTING TIPS!

Who's best to play—and what's the best way to play them?

The base roster includes the eight classic characters featured in *Street Fighter II* (not the bosses), plus Cammy and Dee Jay from *Super Street Fighter II*, Juri from *Super Street Fighter IV*, as well as Luke from *Street Fighter V*. There are also six brand-new characters: Kimberly, Manon, Jamie, Marisa, Lily, and JP.

1 Medal with Manon

Manon, a French ballerina and model, is one of the strongest new characters. The secret to using her is command grabs—that's her two special-move throws, Renversé and Manège Doré. These will max out her medals, which make her stronger. And if you're up against Manon, make sure you block them!

2 He's Kenough

Ken has consistently been one of the best classic characters, and he remains a favorite in *Street Fighter 6*. His moves are mostly simple to execute, making him ideal for beginners, and his Quick Dash combined with a medium kick is easy to insert into combos.

FAST FACT

A test version of a VR game called *Street Fighter VR: Shadaloo Enhancement Plan* was launched in Japan in 2023. Players can enter a training arena and fight Ken or Zangief

3

Special agent

■ British military agent Cammy is a risky choice, because her style relies on fast movement and precise attacks—if you leave her open to opponents, you'll get punished. Don't be afraid to use lighter normal attacks, as they have a shorter recovery time—but when you want to do heavier damage, Spiral Arrow and Cannon Spike are effective and quick.

4

Tough as diamonds

■ When taking on less experienced players, the tanklike Italian jewelry designer Marisa is a sound choice—it takes skills and strategy to take her down. Her charged attacks push back opponents even if they block, which can create the opening you need to follow up. Her size makes her easy to hit, so crouch when necessary.

Turtle power

■ On top of the eighteen base characters, four more have been made available as DLC since the game's release—Rashid and Ed from *Street Fighter V*, Akuma from *Super Street Fighter II Turbo*, and a new character, A.K.I. There's also a *Teenage Mutant Ninja Turtles* crossover!

5

Keep your hands clean

■ The strongest of the new characters is chief bad guy JP—but his ease of use doesn't go lower than Hard, so he's not for new players. His long-range attacks are great, so avoid getting drawn into close combat and use feints to confuse opponents. Stunning the enemy with Triglav or Departure also works.

SAMBA DE AMIGO: PARTY CENTRAL

THIS IS WHERE THE PARTY'S AT!

Here's a sequel that's been a long time coming: the original *Samba de Amigo* came out in arcades in 1999, as part of a whole wave of rhythm-based games. Playing as a monkey called Amigo, you shook maracas to the beat and if you did it well, you attracted a crowd (in the game, we mean, but maybe in real life, too). It was ported to the Sega Dreamcast the next year (with special maraca controllers), and is remembered as one of the console's best games; it arrived on the Wii in 2008.

Now it's back, and the action is much the same as ever, but it's been designed to fit today's tech—VR. As well as the Switch version, you can play it on the Meta Quest—it was one of the launch games for the Meta Quest 3.

QUICK TIPS

NO WINDMILL ARMS

■ Don't move your arms too much when playing. The Joy-Cons will still register small movements as correct, so try moving from the wrist rather than the elbow or shoulder.

GET UP TO SPEED

■ When the game speeds up, make sure you watch the middle of the screen, where the rhythm markers come from. Doing this will help you keep track of the order in which you need to hit them in.

KEEP IN TIME WITH THE BEAT

■ Even when playing the minigames, don't forget it's essential to keep your rhythm—no matter what you're doing, this is still a rhythm game!

TOP TUNES

Party Central comes with a base of forty songs, ranging from Bon Jovi to Charli XCX, and several game modes including a story mode that sees Amigo setting out to rescue lost music.

LITE'S NOT LIT

In the Switch version, the Joy-Cons are your maracas. If you've got a Switch Lite, which doesn't have Joy-Cons, you can use button presses—but this makes the game trickier and it's not as much fun.

SHAKE IT OFF

Multiplayer is a big part of the appeal, and the modes include World Party, an online battle royale played over three rounds—with *Mario Kart*–style weapons to use against opponents!

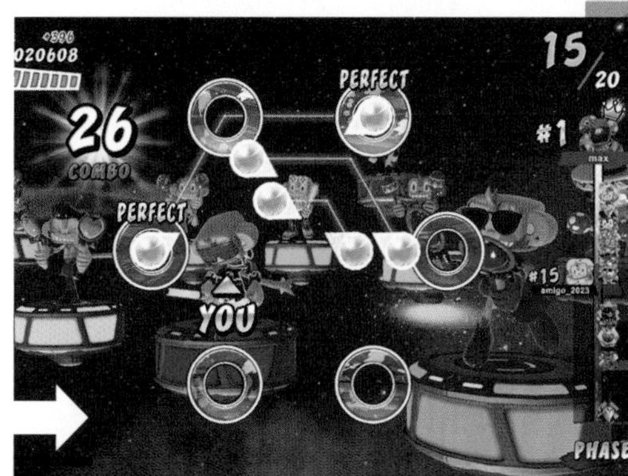

HEART BEAT

Perhaps the best party mode is Love Checker, a co-op mode where you and a friend must stay in sync (the heart at the top closes up when you do) and strike poses!

SONIC BOOM

Sonic features a lot in this game—there's a stage where you and Sonic dance side by side, and some classic music and sound effects from the *Sonic* games are included!

FAST FACT

The original *Samba de Amigo* was made by Sonic Team and the final design for Amigo was done by Yuji Uekawa, the character designer for the Sonic games.

LIKE THIS? TRY THIS:

TAIKO NO TATSUJIN RHYTHM FESTIVAL

Annoyingly, the previous game in this cute, colorful drumming series, *Taiko no Tatsujin: Drum 'n' Fun!*, has been taken off the Nintendo store, so we're recommending the more recent *Rhythm Festival*. The design is amazing—these are the best rhythm games on the Switch!

TOP 10 FREE-TO-PLAY GAMES

Never be priced out of the market!

■ There have never been so many free experiences available to console gamers—here's a rundown of our favorites, with some tips on how to keep them free. But you don't have to take our word for it—download them and try them out!

10 Dauntless

■ This is a *Monster Hunter*–style action RPG in a trad fantasy setting, and you can play solo or with a crew of up to six. It got off to a shaky start when it was launched, with many complaints about lagging, but has developed well, with an original approach to the battle pass model and some enjoyable social aspects—each week there's a themed fashion competition, with rewards of loot! The only paid-for items are cosmetic ones, so you can easily opt out.

AVAILABLE ON: Nintendo Switch, PS5, PS4, Xbox Series S/X, Xbox One, PC, iOS, Android

09 Fallout Shelter

■ This construction and management game was created mainly to promote the release of *Fallout 4*, but it's developed an audience of its own and hung around. It's open-ended—you're placed in charge of a Vault and must look after the apocalypse survivors inside it. There are microtransactions, but if you're patient you can earn everything without buying it.

AVAILABLE ON: PS4, Xbox One, PC, iOS, Android

08 World of Tanks

■ The perfect game for military history enthusiasts on a tight budget, *World of Tanks* covers tank-based warfare up to the Cold War. It's got a lot of depth for a free game, and while it can be daunting at first, the more you learn, the better you get at it. You can pay to unlock premium vehicles and progress faster. You can also check out the air- and sea-based versions, *World of Warplanes* and *World of Warships*.

AVAILABLE ON: Nintendo Switch, PS5, PS4, Xbox Series S/X, Xbox One, PC, Mac, iOS, Android

07 Pinball FX

■ The *Pinball FX* series has been running for many years, but this reboot—made under a partnership with Epic Games—is free-to-play on all the major platforms. It's a pinball simulator; there really isn't much more to explain than that, but the tables are well-designed and feel real, and trying to beat your high score (and other people's) is incredibly addictive. There are three free tables: you can buy more in the store, and some of them are very tempting, but for a quick blast the free version is perfect.

AVAILABLE ON: Nintendo Switch, PS5, PS4, Xbox Series S/X, Xbox One, PC

06 Brawlhalla

■ *Brawlhalla* is a fighting game along the lines of *Super Smash Bros.*, with a range of playable fighters including crossovers with *Adventure Time*, *Street Fighter*, and others. You have to buy premium Mammoth Coins to get the crossover characters, but there's a rotating choice of fighters you can play for free. Your favorite won't always be available, but that just means you'll have to get good at playing with all of them!

AVAILABLE ON: Nintendo Switch, PS5, PS4, Xbox Series S/X, Xbox One, PC, iOS, Android

04 Smite

■ This MMO battle arena game has been around for a decade now, and is a great introduction to the genre, being both free and easy to pick up for newbies. As such it's consistently ranked among the top free-to-play games out there. It's another one that uses the rotating-character method of encouraging players to pay, as only a dozen of its Gods are available at any given time—but if you don't mind that, you're good to go!

AVAILABLE ON: Nintendo Switch, PS4, Xbox One, PC, Mac

05 Fall Guys

■ Epic Games are the kings of free-to-play and *Fall Guys* has benefited from becoming part of their stable. This goofy minigame battle offers lots of frantic fun, and it's had some cool tie-ins like *Doctor Who* skins. One of the benefits of going free is the average match isn't quite as challenging as it used to be, so you have more of a chance!

AVAILABLE ON: Nintendo Switch, PS5, PS4, Xbox Series S/X, Xbox One, PC

03 Genshin Impact

■ In many ways this is a clone of *The Legend of Zelda: Breath of the Wild*—which is one of the best games ever made, so it's not a bad place to take inspiration from. But its gradually revealed map and lore, as well as its smart party-based combat system, have made it an experience players keep coming back to. It makes money via its gacha system—collecting better characters is hard work if you take the free route—but it's perfectly possible to progress with the standard characters.

AVAILABLE ON: PS5, PS4, PC, iOS, Android

02 Rocket League

■ *Rocket League* was already a huge hit even before it went free-to-play in 2020—it's still one of the biggest things in e-sports, with huge cash prizes at the major tournaments—and it's only gotten bigger since then. It's also great that you no longer need to subscribe to your console's online service to play. It shouldn't work at all, really—getting any control over the ball is incredibly frustrating—but somehow it's massively addictive! It's also very easy to spend no money on it.

AVAILABLE ON: Nintendo Switch, PS4, Xbox One, PC, Mac

01 Fortnite

■ *Fortnite* is a free-to-play empire these days—the battle royale mode is the center of it all, of course, but there's *LEGO Fortnite*, *Fortnite Festival*, limited-time experiences, user-made experiences, and good old *Save the World*. They've stuck to the principle of paid-for items being purely cosmetic—you can't buy your way to being better at the game—and you can get a small amount of free V-Bucks each season, which will eventually pay for a Battle Pass. And when you've got the Battle Pass, you can earn more than enough each season to buy the next one!

AVAILABLE ON: Nintendo Switch, PS4, PS5, Xbox One, Xbox Series S/X, PC, iOS, Android

FAST FACT

***Fortnite* got its name from the original *Save the World* missions that lasted fourteen days—the word "fortnight" isn't used much in North America, but is a common British term for "two weeks."**

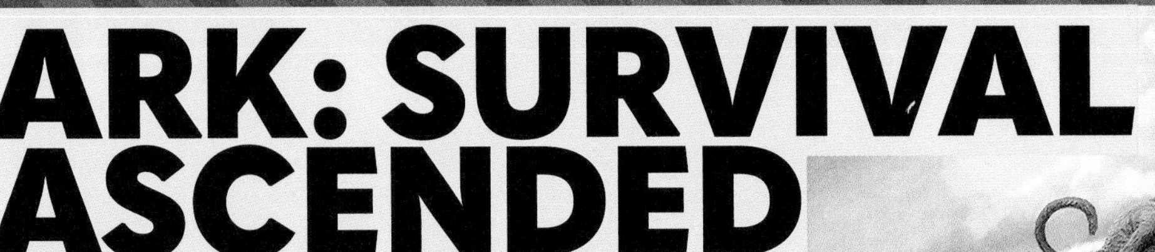

ARK: SURVIVAL ASCENDED

Tame dinosaurs—or get eaten by them!

This isn't a sequel to the 2017 game *ARK: Survival Evolved*—it's a remake of it. It's an open-world game where you play a puny human in a world of dinosaurs, and at first you just have to do what you can to survive. But as it goes on, you can capture those dinosaurs and tame them, with the aim of reaching the top of the food chain!

CLAWS OUT

■ A less well-known dino that makes a killer companion is *Therizinosaurus*—a long-taloned beast that's absolutely deadly! And who can resist building a mobile base on the back of a *Brontosaurus*? This is what we play *ARK* for!

JUST DON'T DIE

■ *ARK* starts off like a hi-res *Minecraft*—you drop into the world with nothing at all, and must craft essential tools and weapons while steering clear of danger until you can cope with it. It can be a pretty tough game!

FAST FACT

There's now an animated series based on *ARK*, following an Australian paleontologist called Helen Walker who washes up on a remote island inhabited by dinosaurs. Guest stars include Vin Diesel, Michelle Yeoh, and David Tennant!

KING OF THE BEASTS

As you may have guessed, the *Tyrannosaurus Rex* is the game's strongest dinosaur, capable of taking down any of the others. They're also good to ride—not the fastest, but they can cope with any terrain.

EVERYTHING'S AN EXPERIENCE

Almost everything you do helps you level up, and as you level up you enhance your stats and unlock new blueprints. If you can find Explorer Notes, this will grant double XP for a limited time, so do as much as you can while boosted!

PIKMIN 4

THE STRATEGY-AND-EXPLORATION SERIES FINALLY CRASH-LANDS ON THE SWITCH!

Pikmin could only have come from Nintendo—a game based around exploring an environment with a sense of wonder, involving gameplay mechanics no one else has thought of. Nintendo has left long gaps between games in this series, always striving to come back with something fresh—and the Switch was already five years old when it finally got a *Pikmin* game.

These games are about as experimental as cute games aimed at an all-ages audience get, and not everything they try works—*Pikmin 3* was probably the weakest of the series. But *Pikmin 4* puts that right with new mechanics and a fab battle mode, and might be the best one yet.

QUICK TIPS

COLOR MATCHING
■ Pikmin should carry pellets of the same color they are. If the Pikmin and pellet match, the pellet will sprout two Pikmin rather than just one.

GET CHATTING
■ Talk to everyone at the base camp—there are lots of side quests to be had, and often these give rewards for things you're doing anyway.

SPEED DEMON
■ When you get the Charging Horn from Russ, you can send all your Pikmin to the same spot. This is great for speeding up play when larger tasks come up.

RESCUE THE RESCUERS

■ This time around, you play as a new recruit to the intergalactic Rescue Corps, tasked with rescuing a rescue party that's been sent to rescue Captain Olimar (from the original game). Both ships have been stranded on an Earthlike planet...

ASSEMBLE THE TROOPS

■ As usual, you have a squad of tiny Pikmin you can command as you explore and try to rescue everyone. It's not the trickiest game—you can rewind time if you make a mistake—but its puzzles are so creative, it's a joy to discover them.

GOING UNDERGROUND

■ *Pikmin 3* removed the "dungeon" areas from *Pikmin 2*—but they're back in this game. These add a nice change of pace, as the gameplay is more directed and they're a little more challenging.

A WONDERFUL WORLD

■ We're pretty used to games with detailed graphics by now, but *Pikmin 4* is still one of the best we've seen. It's so beautifully designed, and the whole world is great to spend time in.

BATTLE STATIONS

■ The co-op mode isn't the greatest, but the new Dandori Battles are great. You can play these little bursts of warfare solo, but they're excellent two-player games.

FAST FACT

Pikmin 4 was confirmed to be in the works in September 2015, when its creator Shigeru Miyamoto said it was "very close to completion." It finally came out almost eight years later!

LIKE THIS? TRY THIS:

KATAMARI DAMACY REROLL

■ There are several games with a similar "command tiny creatures" mechanic, like *Tinykin* and *The Wild at Heart*, but *Katamari Damacy REROLL* is an action puzzle game with its own quirky concept—you roll a sticky ball to collect objects.

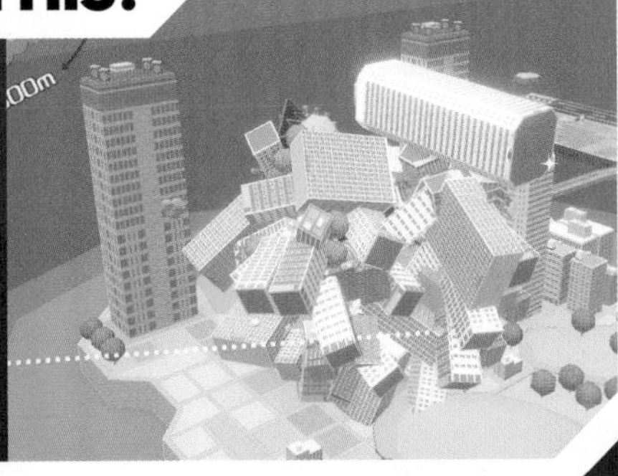

PIKMIN 4: GUIDE TO OATCHI!

Get the hero info and the tips you need to triumph.

OK, so the star of this game is clearly Oatchi, a rescue dog-type-thing belonging to Captain Shepherd, who you find on Day 1. Oatchi joins your mission and is nice to have around—not just because he's cute, but also because he can do things you can't.

1 New tricks

■ The first thing you should do on Day 2 is go to Shepherd and trigger the Oatchi training side mission. Now you'll be able to upgrade Oatchi's abilities, of which there are many: he can sniff things out, jump to high places, break certain objects, and transport you and the Pikmin around the map.

FAST FACT

Like *Pokémon*, *Pikmin* has a free-to-play augmented reality mobile game, *Pikmin Bloom*. It's like a fitness app that's been turned into a game. It rewards you for going outside and walking around.

2 Get buff

■ However, upgrades cost Pup Drive points, so you need to earn them by rescuing castaways and completing Night Expeditions. You can work on the skills that suit your gameplay, but Buff is a good one to get first. This increases Oatchi's strength so he can move and carry things.

Top gear

After rescuing Russ from Last-Frost Cavern, you can buy the gear and items he makes in exchange for raw material. This includes gear for Oatchi, such as protection from fire, freezing, and electrocution. Sniff Saver means he can neutralize poison, and other gear increases his HP and decreases the damage he takes.

3

4

What a rush

Rush is also important, as this means Oatchi can break things and charge at enemies. You may wish to upgrade both of these further, to Super Buff and Mega Rush. Other handy things include Doggy Paddle, which means Oatchi can swim and carry you across water; Chomp, a biting attack; and Swallow, which lets him carry things in his mouth.

Highly advanced

The Stone of Advancement, a treasure you collect from the Rescue Command Post, is actually a Game Boy Advance SP, a Nintendo handheld console from the early 2000s. Nintendo's Yuji Kando says, "It'd be nice if parents and children had conversations like, 'Mum, Dad, what's this?' 'I had one of those back in the day. Want to know how I played it?'"

RIDE 5

BE THE FASTEST THING ON TWO WHEELS!

Motorcycle racing games used to have an arcade-y style, focusing on being fast and fun rather than deeply realistic. But the *Ride* series shows how the genre has gone in a different direction. In these, you can really feel the weight of the bike, and pushing down the accelerator and leaning hard into corners won't get you very far. This game wants you to know what it's really like to ride.

Because of this, it won't be for everyone—it's tricky to pick up and there isn't much in the way of help when you start the game. But it looks incredibly realistic, making full use of the latest hardware (it's only on PC, PS5, and Xbox Series X/S), and the gameplay matches up to it!

QUICK TIPS

GO AUTOMATIC

■ Complete newcomers to *Ride* should turn on auto brakes to begin with—this will brake the correct amount to turn corners. However, disabling joint brakes or brake input modulation will make the game very tough!

GET ON THE RIGHT PATH

■ The closest thing to a tutorial is the ideal trajectory option, which will show you the best racing line to take—there's also an option to just have this on corners.

STAND TRIAL

■ Practice in time trial to start with—you need to learn how to handle the bike before you start thinking about racing against anyone else—and Monza or Brands Hatch are good starter circuits.

RACE TO THE TOP

Don't be surprised if you get a *Gran Turismo* vibe from *Ride 5*—this series is very much aiming to do for bikes what *Gran Turismo* has done for cars.

GRANULAR DETAIL

The detail of the circuits is remarkable—the texture of the road, the tire tracks on the road, even the grimy bits at the bottom of the curb. It almost looks like a photo!

GREAT SHAKES

Racing games are perfect for DualShock—the controller can help give you a real sense of how your vehicle is handling, and *Ride 5* does this extremely well.

POWER UP . . . AND UP

There's a lot of playing time in the new Career Mode—you start out with the lowest-powered 250cc bikes and work your way up to the 1000cc ones. Given how hard the game is, playing this way is pretty sensible!

CALM IT DOWN

You may want to experiment with the collisions and CPU opponent settings, because other racers can get aggressive and knock you off your bike! If you want to just focus on racing, tone that stuff down.

FAST FACT

The developer of the *Ride* series, Milestone, is based in Italy and also makes the *Hot Wheels Unleashed* games, if you want a less intense racing experience.

LIKE THIS? TRY THIS:

MOTOGP 23

The official game of the *MotoGP* series has a similar difficulty level to *Ride 5*, which might put off casual gamers, but it's got a great career mode, including trash-talking social media posts from your rivals!

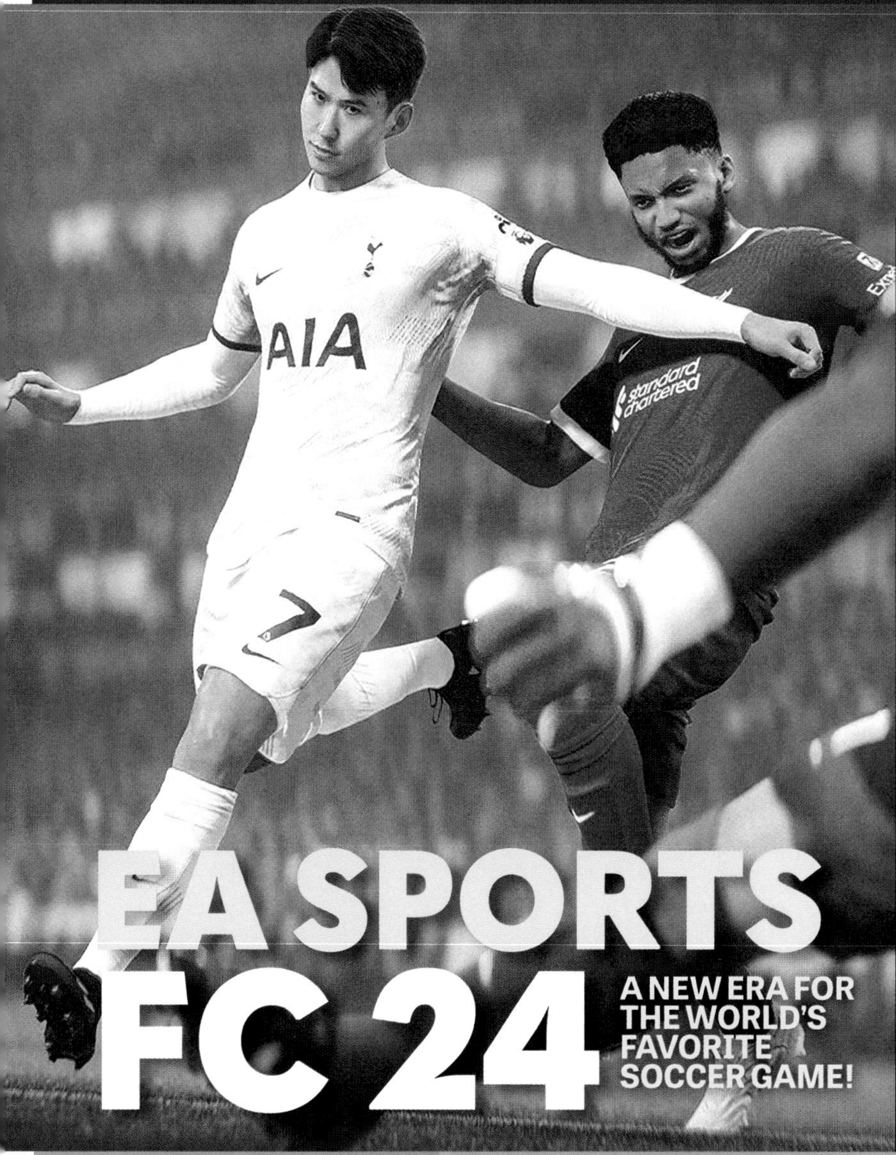

EA SPORTS FC 24

A NEW ERA FOR THE WORLD'S FAVORITE SOCCER GAME!

EA's soccer games have carried the official FIFA license since the very first game back in 1993 . . . until now. EA has struck out on its own, and the series is simply called *EA Sports FC*.

This decision actually makes a lot of sense. Over the years EA has collected dozens of official licenses for teams and competitions, and these are more important to players than the FIFA license. The game still feels like it's got everything *FIFA* used to have except an extra World Cup mode every four years (and you can easily make your own World Cup in Custom Tournament).

EA Sports FC has seen off challenges from rivals like *Pro Evolution Soccer*. It's slick and refined and has more real teams with real kits and real players than any other game. It's hard to see anything beating it now!

QUICK TIPS

JOCKEY FOR POSITION

■ Defending well in these games is always a challenge. Jockeying is a good skill to learn—there's a whole tutorial on defensive skills, and you can put them to the test in a practice match.

TAKE ON NEW FORMATIONS

■ Set up different formations you can switch between. It's well worth the effort—one for attack, one for defense (try 4-2-3-1 for this), and a more balanced one.

KEEP YOUR SHAPE

■ Try not to make your defenders chase the ball too much—it's important to keep them in position and let your midfielders do the running. If a defender gets out of position, the opposition will usually exploit the gap very quickly.

WHAT'S NEW?

If you know *FIFA*, you know what this game is like—and if you don't know *FIFA*, it's like soccer. You can play standard 11v11 or Volta formats with smaller teams on smaller pitches. But what did they bring in for *FC 24*?

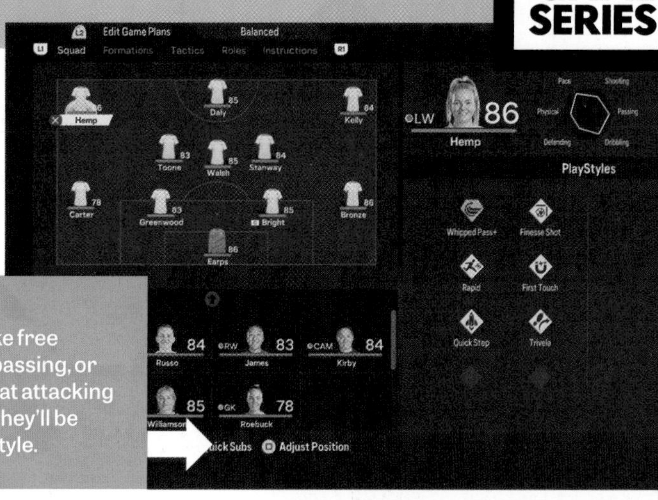

PLAYSTYLES

To make players in the game better reflect how they play in real life, *FC 24* includes Playstyles. So if a player is particularly good at something like free kicks, tiki-taka passing, or anticipating what attacking players will do, they'll be given that Playstyle.

PRECISION PASSING

This is a new type of passing, where instead of using the usual player-targeting system, you can choose the space you want to pass the ball into by holding down the right shoulder button.

NEW LEAGUES

EA has been slow to expand its roster of women's teams, but *FIFA 23* included women's club sides for the first time—and *FC 24* adds the women's leagues from Spain and Germany. However, a big loss from the national sides is Brazil—the men's and women's teams!

EVERYONE'S INCLUDED IN ULTIMATE

Ultimate Team has always had a fantasy aspect, with the ability to add legendary players from the past to your squad. Now you can field a team mixing male and female players!

FAST FACT

Another new license picked up by EA is the Ballon d'Or, a prize awarded to the world's best footballer each year. This is now the ultimate prize in Career Mode—level up and play consistently very, very well and you may have a chance!

LIKE THIS? TRY THIS:

PRO EVOLUTION SOCCER 5

The Ultimate Team mode of *FC 24* is a little like the Master League mode from this game—but Master League is just more satisfying! You control a team of low-quality players and—this is where the "evolution" part comes in—make them better through playing and training.

MADDEN NFL 24

ANOTHER IN THE LEGENDARY FOOTBALL SERIES TOUCHES DOWN!

The original *John Madden Football* came out way back in 1988, and set new standards of realism in sports games. EA became the biggest name in the genre because of this series, and while some fans feel it's fallen behind other sports games in recent years, it's in no danger of losing its crown as the leading football game.

One exciting thing about the *24* edition—minigames are back! These were dropped after *Madden NFL 13*, but they're a great way for newcomers to learn and they're fun for everyone else. They're an essential part of evolving your players' skills in the Superstar, Franchise, and Training Camp modes, so if that's the way you want to play, you'll be playing these minigames a lot!

QUICK TIPS

PICK YOUR POSITION

Be careful about taking control of your backfield defenders—if they end up out of position, you can get into trouble very quickly. Your defensive ends are better players to work with.

TIME TO WIN

If you're winning, look for ways to run down the clock toward the end of the game and just generally keep possession of the ball. The opposition can't score if they don't have it!

THIS TOO WILL PASS

Learn all the different types of passes. Start by focusing on the bullet pass—its speed means it reaches the receiver more reliably—but then work on the others.

WHAT'S NEW?

Madden NFL 23 gave its on-the-field action a welcome push forward, and that continues in *24*. While the return of minigames will grab people's attention, it's the gameplay itself that's really improved in this edition.

LOOKING GOOD

The graphics have taken a step forward—there's more variety in the animation and the players have been reworked to improve their movement. It's spookily realistic!

LET'S CELEBRATE

This includes the players' celebrations. Sports games can feel repetitive when the same reactions keep coming up, but *Madden* is now stocked with enough that it'll keep on surprising you.

TAKE THE HIT

There are over 1,700 new or reworked animations for tackles in *Madden NFL 24*, and the impacts are really strong—you feel it when you take someone down!

SMART GUYS

AI in sports games is making big leaps, and you can see this in *Madden*'s defenses—if you try the same play a few times in a row, they'll learn and close it down more quickly.

FAST FACT

John Madden's playing career was cut short by injury before he played a professional game, but he went on to become a highly successful coach, then a TV commentator—which led to him being asked to work on *John Madden Football*.

LIKE THIS? TRY THIS:

MUTANT FOOTBALL LEAGUE

Inspired by an old Mega Drive game called *Mutant League Football* that used the same engine as *Madden*, this is 7v7 football played by skeletons, demons, aliens, and werewolves. Just the thing if you need a break from *Madden*'s intense realism!

NBA 2K24

THE TOP BASKETBALL GAME BOUNCES BACK FOR ANOTHER EDITION!

Ironically, there's not a lot of competition in the world of sports games these days. Most sports have a leading video game that holds the official licenses, meaning they have all the real players, teams, and stadiums—and that's the game everyone wants. The *NBA 2K* series dominates basketball, and it brings the sport to gaming perfectly.

Players should be wary, however, of the microtransactions in some game modes. MyCareer can be a frustrating experience unless you're willing to do a lot of grinding or spend extra on upgrades. Your player will be pretty mid, and you'll find it hard work to beat players who've spent money to be better. This kind of thing is OK in free-to-play games, but with a premium title like this, it's annoying to say the least.

QUICK TIPS

TAKE AIM

Getting "green" shots in this edition is easier, and so is shooting from behind the halfway line. It's not exactly realistic, but worth a try if you don't have other options!

YOU GOT THE MOVES

The best dribble style to equip is Kyrie Irving. Use Steve Francis for Signature Size-Up, Isaiah Thomas for Regular Breakdown Combo, and Jamal Murray for Aggressive Breakdown Combo.

GET IN THE WAY

When defending, disrupt opponents when they have the ball. Even if you don't win it back, this will cause them to lose their adrenaline boost.

WHAT'S NEW?

Like *Madden*, the best improvements in *NBA 2K24* are very much about the on-court action. It's better-looking and smarter, than ever—and while *2K23* covered the world around basketball, this game has pulled back on that to focus more on the sport itself.

A SANDBOX BY THE BEACH

MyCareer still has some nice stuff that expands beyond the court—The City is a sandbox environment you can wander around in and find side quests, or play 3v3 on the beachfront.

THAT'S PRO

A new feature called ProPLAY enables developers to scan real-life footage of players and use it to make animations in the game—which makes movements feel more human.

THAT'S THE GUY!

This is backed up by the behavior of players—when you're up against the NBA's most famous stars, their style feels right for that player.

ROBOT REWARD

There are some pretty crazy things you can earn by playing through the Season Pass, like random mascot costumes and this awesome Chrome Cyborg suit!

FAST FACT

This is the fourth *NBA 2K* game to feature Kobe Bryant on its cover, including the special edition of *2K21* that was released after his death in a helicopter crash at the age of 41.

LIKE THIS? TRY THIS:

NBA JAM

This 2v2 version of basketball was wildly popular in arcades in the 1990s, and was a hit on home consoles too. It's still a fast, fun way to play basketball—especially for those who don't know much about the sport!

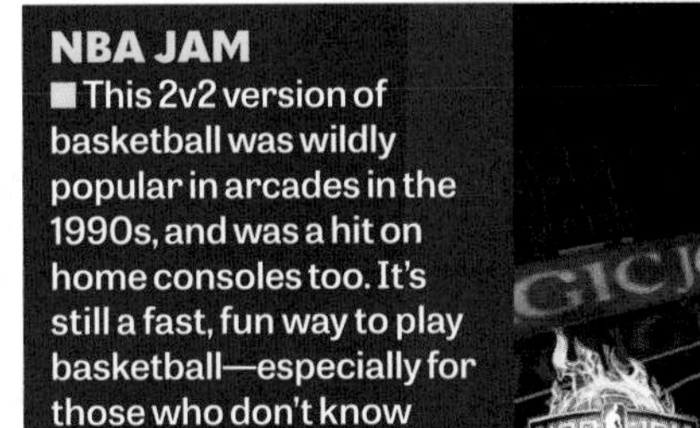

Princess Peach: Showtime!

Play a game about a play!

■ Princess Peach has usually been the helpless damsel in distress of the *Mario* series. Although games such as *Super Mario Bros. 2* and *Super Mario 3D World* have featured her as a playable character, her standard role from *Super Mario Bros.* to *Super Mario Odyssey* has been to get kidnapped by Bowser, requiring Mario to rescue her.

Her only starring role on a Nintendo console came way back in 2005 with *Super Princess Peach* on the DS. But the *Super Mario Bros.* movie showcased a tougher, more active Peach, without losing her innate princess quality—and *Princess Peach: Showtime!*, her first solo outing on the Switch, follows it up perfectly.

Play off

■ In this adventure, Peach goes to see a play at the Sparkle Theater—which is then taken over by a new villain, the wicked Grape and her minions, the Sour Bunch. Peach resolves to save the day with the help of Stella, guardian of the theater.

FAST FACT

The first-ever solo Princess Peach game wasn't on a Nintendo console at all—it was an LCD game watch called *Princess Toadstool's Castle Run* (or just *Peach* in Japan), released by Nelsonic Industries in 1990.

Weird weapon

■ Stella's magic green ribbon becomes Peach's weapon—she can spin it around herself and use it like a whip, fetching coins and striking at the Sour Bunch. This is just one way *Showtime!* displays the creativity we're used to from *Mario* games.

Play the part

■ But the real fun begins when Peach ventures into the different plays that have been taken over by the Sour Bunch. She takes on different roles in these—so Swordfighter Peach has a musketeer outfit and tackles enemies with a rapier.

Get a clue

■ As Peach moves between plays, the game switches between genres—so there's a segment where Peach dresses like Sherlock Holmes and turns detective, investigating thefts from a museum, and another where she must become Patissiere Peach and replace desserts that have been stolen from a sweets festival.

Peach punch

■ Meanwhile Kung Fu Peach is the character she takes on to liberate a martial arts school that's been taken over by the Sour Bunch! And there's more to discover as the game goes on …

DRAGON QUEST MONSTERS: THE DARK PRINCE

YOU COME FOR THE KING, YOU BETTER NOT MISS...

The *Dragon Quest* RPG series dates way back to the 1980s—the first game came out on the NES in 1986. The *Monsters* spin-off line started in 1998, with monster designs by *Dragon Ball* creator Akira Toriyama, and has been hugely successful in Japan—but *The Dark Prince* is the first in the series to get a worldwide release since *Dragon Quest Monsters: Joker 2* back in 2011.

The Dark Prince slots into *Dragon Quest* lore just before the events of Dragon *Quest IV: Chapters of the Chosen*, depicting the origin of Manslayer from that game—or Psaro as he was known back then. But don't worry—if you're new to the series, it's all pretty clear!

QUICK TIPS

KNOW WHEN TO GO LARGE

■ Large monsters can get two or more actions per turn—but they also take up two slots, and won't have as much health as two smaller monsters. So use them strategically!

IMPROVE YOUR REPUTATION

■ After you defeat a region's boss, your reputation in that area goes up. This means when you return to that region, scouting will become easier—so it's worth going back!

FOCUS YOUR ATTACKS

■ Concentrate on one enemy at a time during battles, to reduce the number you have to fight. Attacks that damage multiple enemies at once are best used when one of them is close to being taken out.

A REVENGE MISSION

The plot of *The Dark Prince* is surprisingly, well, dark. Psaro's mother is human and his father Randolfo is a monster and king of the Underworld, Nadiria. Randolfo has hexed Psaro to make him harmless to other monsters. That's why Psaro has become a monster trainer—he needs them so he can return and take on his father . . .

GOTTA SCOUT THEM ALL

The monsters have similarities to Pokémon—though monster-collecting has been part of the main series games since before *Pokémon* began, and *Dragon Quest Monsters* adds elements of its own. Basically you scout and collect monsters, pitch them into battles, and tackle bosses.

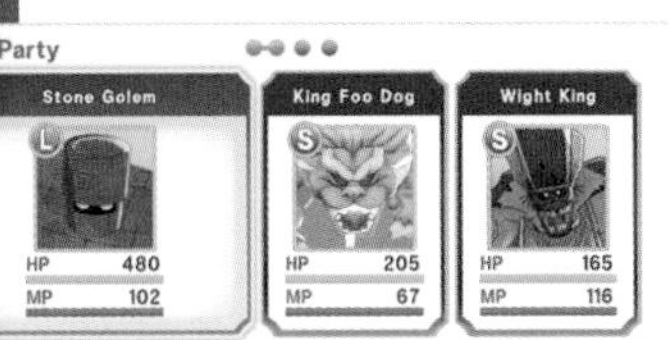

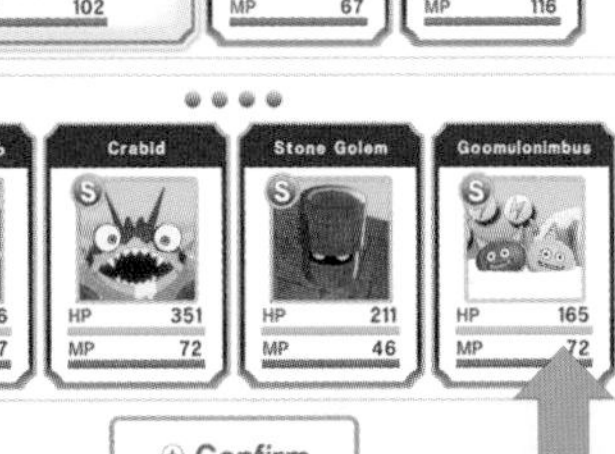

BACK INTO BATTLE

Battling with your monsters makes them level up—and you'll get some progression from almost every battle. This makes the game nicely addictive—there's always the urge to do one more battle and level up another of your monsters.

SWITCH IT UP

Don't just find a favorite lineup and stick with it. The best players change their party regularly. Look at the strengths and weaknesses of the opposition and find the most effective monsters to counter them with.

WILD AND WACKY

The *Dragon Quest Monsters* series is known for its quirky, sometimes downright goofy designs—and as you can see, they've resisted the temptation to go for a more slick, detailed look.

FAST FACT

The first few *Dragon Quest* games were called *Dragon Warrior* outside Japan, because there was a tabletop RPG similar to *Dungeons & Dragons* called *DragonQuest*. But that game is no longer around, so the games can be called *Dragon Quest* everywhere.

LIKE THIS? TRY THIS:

DRAGON QUEST XI S: ECHOES OF AN ELUSIVE AGE—DEFINITIVE EDITION

If you've never checked out the main series, this remaster of the 2017 game *Echoes of an Elusive Age* is a great place to start—it was designed to expand the series' audience beyond Japan, and is rated as one of the best.

DO THE MONSTER MASH-UP!

One of the most important elements of *The Dark Prince* is its synthesis system, which allows you to fuse two monsters to create a new one. This is what gives the game real depth, providing plenty for players to discover—but it's also pretty essential to progress!

Synthesis

Reverse Search

Choose parent monsters to impart their essence, creating a brand new monster.

STAT TRICK

You learn synthesis at the Altar of Amalgamation. The stats of your new monster will be a quarter of the combined stats of the two parent monsters—so it'll be weaker at first, but the better the parents, the stronger the new monster. It will have half the combined skill points.

Fire Chief

Available Traits and Skills

Flame Slash

Flame Breath

Firebird acquires the following traits and skills:

Scorch

Ultra Frizz Ward

OK

TALENT SCOUT

Monsters caught in the wild, even of the same type, won't be as strong as ones you've synthesized yourself. Synthesized monsters have three talents and three hundred talent points, whereas scouted monsters only have two talents and two hundred points. You'll need monsters of this strength—without them, the later stages of the game will be a real challenge!

TAKING A SHINE

Also, monsters you scout will never be shiny. Shiny monsters have higher stats and can only be acquired by synthesis—and even then, they only happen rarely. If you use a shiny monster as a parent for another synthesis, the resulting fusion will not be shiny—so hang on to them!

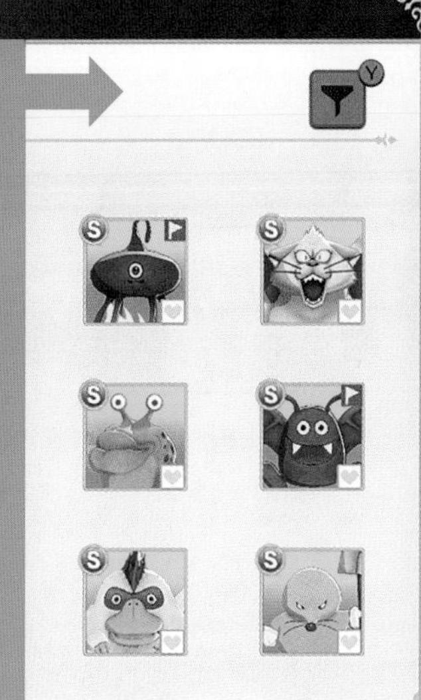

FUSIONS TO USE

■ In the early part of the game, the best fusions to acquire are Raptile (synthesize Vegandragora and Bag o' Laughs), Cannonbrawler (Bodkin Archer and Mecha-Mynah), Hunter Mech (Restless Armor and any Material), Mandrake Major (Restless Armor and Raptile), Axesaurus (Mandrake Major and any Material), Warhog (Mandrake Major and any Beast), and Dessert Demon (Imp and Chocolate Golem).

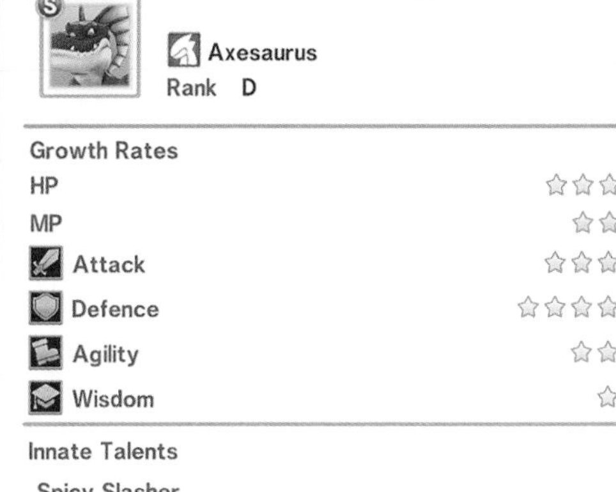

FAST FACT

***Dragon Quest* also has its own *Pokémon Go* type geolocation mobile game, *Dragon Quest Walk*, which is free to play on Android and iOS.**

ALL FOUR YOU

■ You can also do four-monster synthesis by taking two synthesized monsters and fusing them to create another. Prism Peacock is an example of this, requiring a fusion of Firebird, Phoenix, Snowbird, and Gangleclaw—you could call them Prism Peacock's grandparents. Other four-monster fusions include Greater Platypink and Balhib.

RAD REMAKES, REBOOTS, AND REMASTERS

Great games made even greater with a fresh coat of paint!

Old games used to get left behind when their platform got replaced by a newer, more powerful one. The games world moved on to slicker, faster games with more detailed graphics and crunchier sound. The thinking was "Who'd want to play those creaky old games now?"

But, gameplay has always been the most important thing, and sometimes a great game is just a great game. Some gamers are happy to play the originals in all their retro glory—but sometimes, what a classic game needs to reach a whole new audience is spruced-up graphics, re-recorded dialogue—and maybe some tweaks for that glitchy level that irked everyone the first time around. We explore some of the great games that have been brought back to life on newer platforms!

THE LEGEND OF ZELDA: LINK'S AWAKENING

ORIGINAL: 1993
REMAKE: 2019

■ There are always new *Zelda* fans looking to explore its past, as well as old fans looking to relive it. The HD remaster of *Skyward Sword*, with its crucial lore revelations, was a hit, but the Switch version of *Link's Awakening* from the Game Boy was even more ambitious. In bringing this game to a home console for the first time, the developers introduced a whole new cute, toylike visual style, giving it a very different feel from recent *Zelda* games—and a brand new create-your-own-dungeon feature!

GRIM FANDANGO REMASTERED

ORIGINAL: 1998
REMAKE: 2014, 2015, 2018, 2020

In this adventure game, you play "travel agent" Manny Calavera, who guides the souls of the dead to the afterlife. It flopped on its original release, perhaps because it's rock hard—it's rarely obvious how you're meant to progress—but its design, writing, and voice acting are some of the best you'll ever see, even if its 3D polygon animation looks basic now. It has gradually been released across all current-gen platforms, though you might need a walkthrough guide on hand!

FINAL FANTASY VII REMAKE

ORIGINAL: 1997
REMAKE: 2020

The seventh game in the *Final Fantasy* series was regarded as one of the best, but games from the early 3D era can be a struggle to play now. The developers of the series, Square Enix, decided to remake the entire thing from scratch, expanding the story and turning it into three games! Also see our feature on the second part, *Final Fantasy VII Rebirth*.

TONY HAWK'S PRO SKATER 1 + 2

ORIGINAL: 1999, 2000
REMAKE: 2020, 2021

The *Tony Hawk* games were a phenomenon on the PlayStation and PS2, due to their perfect physics, cleverly designed environments, and gnarly punk and hip-hop soundtracks. The remastered bundle of the first two games polishes the graphics and adds moves introduced later in the series. It can be frustrating trying to hit those high scores, but you'll keep going for another round, then another . . . then another. Don't touch the disastrous *Tony Hawk's Pro Skater 5*, this is what you need!

SUPER MONKEY BALL BANANA MANIA

ORIGINAL: 2001, 2002, 2005
REMAKE: 2021

■ *Banana Mania* bundles together everything from the first three *Super Monkey Ball* games, including more than three hundred levels, but also updates them. Like most classic arcade games, *Super Monkey Ball* gave you limited lives, forcing you to keep paying if you wanted to keep playing, and home console versions would usually work the same way—but today's home gamers don't want to keep starting over again, and so *Banana Mania* gives you infinite attempts to master each stage!

METROID PRIME REMASTERED

ORIGINAL: 2002
REMAKE: 2023

■ The GameCube's first *Metroid* game was one of the biggest sellers on the console. It was the first in the series to use 3D graphics and a first-person perspective—and is still one of the top-rated games of all time. So a Switch remaster makes perfect sense, and it has been improved by overhauling the control system as well as updating the visuals.

MARIO VS. DONKEY KONG

ORIGINAL: 2004
REMAKE: 2024

■ The Game Boy Advance puzzle platformer *Mario vs. Donkey Kong* pitted Mario against his original archenemy, and became a successful branch of the *Mario* family tree, with a whopping five sequels. This remaster of the original brings it into line with other recent *Mario* games—Mario looks like he does in *Super Mario Bros. Wonder*—and adds a welcome two-player co-op mode!

PAPER MARIO: THE THOUSAND-YEAR DOOR

ORIGINAL: 2004
REMAKE: 2024

After the success of the *Super Mario RPG* remake, the logical thing to do would be a remake of the first *Paper Mario* game, which carried over much of the gameplay from *RPG*. But Nintendo wouldn't go along with anything as boring as logic, and instead opted to revisit the second *Paper Mario* game. It's widely reckoned to be the best in the series anyway, so maybe it does make sense!

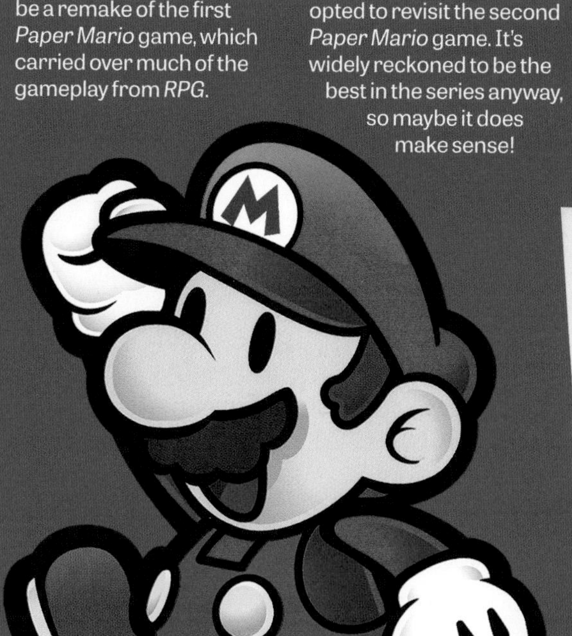

DESTROY ALL HUMANS!

ORIGINAL: 2005
REMAKE: 2020

It's not just mega franchises that can revive their old games for a new audience! The *Destroy All Humans!* games were popular on the PS2 and Xbox in the 2000s, with their retro 1950s sci-fi setting and angry alien protagonist, but they ended in 2008, after the fourth in the series. The 2020 remake got mixed reviews, but was a surprise hit and led to a remake of the second game as well as a multiplayer spin-off, *Clone Carnage*!

ANOTHER CODE: RECOLLECTION

ORIGINAL: 2005, 2009
REMAKE: 2024

Sometimes a remake gives a game another chance in countries where the original never came out. *Another Code: Two Memories* on the DS was a neat point-and-click mystery game, atmospheric and visually rich. It got a sequel on the Wii, *Another Code: R—A Journey into Lost Memories*, which was a slow-burning success in Europe and Japan. However, it never even came out in North America! This excellent remaster puts that right, bundling both games together.

POKÉMON BRILLIANT DIAMOND AND SHINING PEARL

ORIGINAL: 2006
REMAKE: 2021

■ Following on from the *Let's Go!* games, which remade the original *Pokémon Red* and *Pokémon Blue* for the Switch, *Brilliant Diamond* and *Shining Pearl* tackle the fourth generation of handheld *Pokémon* games. It was a little controversial among fans of the series, though, with some loving the reworked 3D visuals and others hating them, and some feeling it had been changed too much, while others said it hadn't been changed enough. A remake rarely pleases everyone!

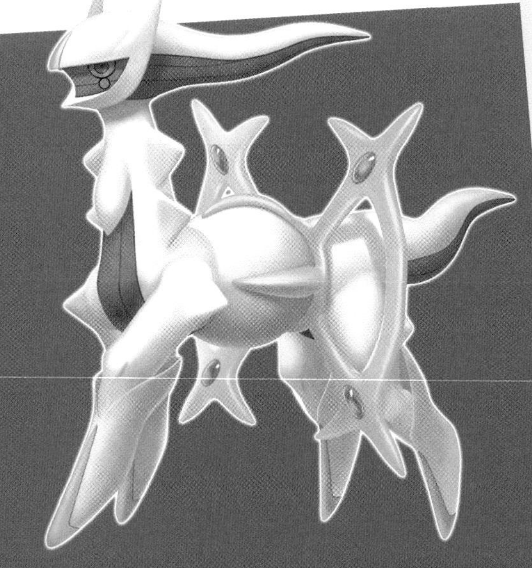

LUIGI'S MANSION 2 HD

ORIGINAL: 2013
REMAKE: 2024

■ These days, with the Switch being both home console and handheld, it's weird to think there were so many Nintendo games that only ever came out on handheld platforms. *Luigi's Mansion: Dark Moon* is a great example—one of the biggest-selling games on the 3DS, but was it a full sequel to *Luigi's Mansion* or not? We've since had *Luigi's Mansion 3*, so now Nintendo has brought *Dark Moon* into line with the others by remaking it for the Switch and calling it *Luigi's Mansion 2*.

BROTHERS: A TALE OF TWO SONS

ORIGINAL: 2013
REMAKE: 2024

■ This beautiful, emotional indie adventure game had a really clever design: it followed two brothers searching for a cure for their father's illness, and each thumbstick controlled a different brother. The original release won awards, and while its storytelling didn't need an upgrade, the PS5 and Xbox X/S remake gives greater depth and details to its graphics, drawing you even further into its world.

MARVEL'S SPIDER-MAN REMASTERED

ORIGINAL: 2018
REMAKE: 2020

■ OK, so it had only been two years since *Spider-Man* came out for the PS4 when it was spruced up for the PS5, alongside the Miles Morales spin-off that used the same map. But it seems likely we'll see more of this in the future: it's becoming normal for new consoles to work with the previous generation of games, and offering gamers an upgrade on their games as well as their console makes sense!

NICKELODEON ALL-STAR BRAWL 2

MORE CARTOON VIOLENCE THAN ANY OTHER GAME!

If you weren't into the first game in this series, it's still worth checking out the sequel. *Nickelodeon All-Star Brawl 2* is the same kind of thing, of course—it's a *Smash Bros.*–style 2D fighter, with characters from cartoons like *Teenage Mutant Ninja Turtles*, *Avatar: The Last Airbender*, *Garfield*, *The Ren & Stimpy Show*, *Rugrats*, and *SpongeBob SquarePants*—but it's all been tuned up and is now a worthy rival to *Smash*.

In fighting games, it's all-important for different fighters to handle differently and for the game to reward mastery of moves and strategy, rather than button-mashing or making the same move over and over again—and this is what the sequel does so well. And it has a new single-player campaign, too!

QUICK TIPS

IN RECOVERY

■ Learn each fighter's recovery moves. These are essential to avoid getting booted off the screen too quickly—and if you know opponents' moves, you can figure out ways to counter them.

HIT THE GROUND

■ Avoid the "grounded" state that happens when you get a big knockback. Either use the shield button to bounce back, or make a move like an aerial, an up special, or an air dodge.

RIDING A WAVE

■ Learn to wave dash. This move happens when you air dodge into the ground, going into a slide from which you can make attacks.

THE TOP TIER

■ Of course, part of the fun of a game like this is being able to play favorite characters—and *All-Star Brawl 2* is pretty balanced, so whoever you play as, you've got a chance of winning. But who, in our opinion, is the best choice?

REPTAR

■ This game doesn't have many big, heavy characters—so Reptar from *Rugrats* is a difficult opponent and good for new players. He's slow but has great recovery, so you're less likely to get blitzed.

EL TIGRE

■ The star of *El Tigre: The Adventures of Manny Rivera* is another quick fighter, and his attacks chain well so it's easy to put combos together. You can play an aggressive game with him and give opponents no time to fight back!

AZULA

■ The *Avatar: The Last Airbender* villain is fast and lively with a projectile-heavy moveset, and her fire attacks create chaos in the arena. Her main weakness is in recovery, so she is recommended only for more experienced players.

SPONGEBOB

■ A good all-around fighter with a varied moveset, SpongeBob is especially effective in the air, with attacks that can hit a big area—such as the karate slice and flip kick.

FAST FACT

Nickelodeon was the first-ever cable network for children, launched in April 1979. Its first three original animated series—*Doug*, *Rugrats*, and *The Ren & Stimpy Show*—all started on the same day in 1991.

LIKE THIS? TRY THIS:

MULTIVERSUS

■ This free-to-play platform fighter is *Smash Bros.* for characters owned by WB, and has a fantastically varied cast of fighters ranging from *Scooby-Doo* to *Suicide Squad*.

ATLAS FALLEN

In which sand gets everywhere.

While gamers were eagerly awaiting the first new proper *Prince of Persia* game in over a decade, a new game stole in a few months ahead of it. *Atlas Fallen*'s desert-based fantasy semi-open world has a definite *Persia* vibe—it's ruled by the evil Sun God, Thelos, where a rebellion is brewing against the oppressive regime. The hero has a mysterious dream, then a powerful being gives them a magic item that will help them on their quest… You know how this goes, right?

PARRY THE FIGHT

■ The combat system takes some getting used to, but learning to parry is very important. Landing hits and parries fills your Momentum Gauge, which in turn unlocks new abilities you've added to your character! Customizing your character in this way gives real depth to the game.

DUNE BUDDIES

■ There's an online co-op option, which is the best way to play the game. You can split up and tackle different quests—any rewards will benefit both of you, regardless of whether you're together, and you can get through a lot of grinding this way.

FAST FACT

Deck13 Interactive, who made *Atlas Fallen*, were also responsible for the soulslike games *Lords of the Fallen* and *The Surge*—but aimed for this one to be a little easier and more accessible than those.

SAND SKIPPING

The movement in this game is excellent, and other games should be looking at it to see how it's done. You can travel by skimming and surfing the sand dunes, as well as leaping between them, and it's all perfectly smooth.

RUN THE GAUNTLET

You're equipped with a gauntlet that gives you power over sand—which is good, because there's a lot of sand about. This is how your weapons are generated—out of the sand—but naturally the gauntlet isn't complete, and needs some upgrades.

SONIC SUPERSTARS

THERE'S LIFE IN THE OLD 'HOG YET!

The co-creator of *Sonic the Hedgehog*, Naoto Ohshima, left the *Sonic* games behind after helping develop the first 3D game in the series, *Sonic Adventure*, in 1998. But he was surprised by the success of the 2017 game *Sonic Mania*, which went right back to the traditional 2D, side-scrolling style of the original *Sonic* games, and decided to come back to *Sonic*.

Sonic Superstars takes that speedy 2D action, but adds a fresh approach to the graphics—the retro pixel style of *Mania* is out, and a slick new cartoon style is in. *Super Mario Bros. Wonder* may have stolen its thunder a bit by going 2D at the same time, but this is *Sonic* at its best!

QUICK TIPS

TAKE IT SLOW
■ It's tempting—and fun!—to go superfast through every level, but take time to explore, get power-ups, coins, and Chaos Emeralds.

TREAURE HUNTER
■ Most acts have four or five hidden coins you can spend in the in-game store. Finding the hidden golden Badnik in each level will earn you a coin!

A-MAZE-ING LOOT!
■ More coins can be won in the maze stages, which are like the special stages from the first *Sonic* game. You access these by hitting a checkpoint with fifty or more rings.

ISLAND GETAWAY

Sonic Superstars is set on the Northstar Islands, famous for the giant creatures who live there. Dr Eggman has a plot to robotize them into huge Badniks—and it's down to Sonic and co. to stop him, as usual.

AMAZING ABILITIES

The four playable characters of *Superstars* all have special skills. Sonic has the Drop Dash created for *Sonic Mania*, while Tails can fly, Amy has a hammer and Double Jump ability, and Knuckles can climb and glide.

FANG CLUB

We've also got the return of Fang the Hunter, first seen in the Game Gear game *Sonic the Hedgehog: Triple Trouble*. He's working for Eggman to steal the Chaos Emeralds—and he has a sidekick…

QUITE A TRIP

Fang is working with a new character, Trip, a sungazer lizard who wears heavy bronze armor. Though she starts off on the side of the bad guys, she goes on quite a journey in this game!

STICK TOGETHER

Up to four of you can play in multiplayer co-op—in which the camera focuses on one player, so everyone else gets left behind a lot. It's a shame they didn't use split screen for this!

FAST FACT

You can get a LEGO-style Sonic skin as free DLC, and there's a digital upgrade featuring more LEGO skins—a nice callback to the *Sonic* add-on from *LEGO Dimensions*!

LIKE THIS? TRY THIS:

CUPHEAD

The look of *Cuphead* may be based on classic cartoons, but the gameplay has the feel of classic *Sonic*, with its fast, spontaneous levels and tricky boss fights. Be warned though: It is tough!

THIS IS MY GEM

Power up your gameplay with these top tips...

The biggest addition to the gameplay of *Superstars* is the introduction of Emerald Powers, which you acquire with each Chaos Emerald you collect. These do things like slow down time, create clones of your character, or grow a vine that lets you reach new areas. After being used, each power needs time to recharge.

1 Don't stop for anything

Race is like it sounds—a test of speed, using a shorter version of one of the main game levels. Knowing the courses well is a big advantage, as you can avoid anything that might slow you down. You can also pick up and deploy *Mario Kart*–style banana skins to trip up opponents.

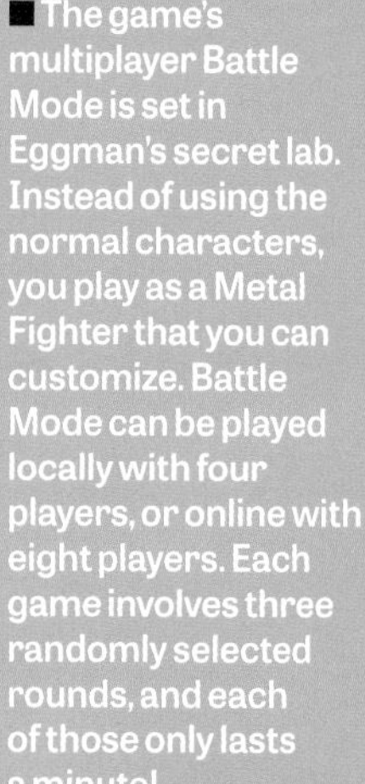

2 Face off

The game's multiplayer Battle Mode is set in Eggman's secret lab. Instead of using the normal characters, you play as a Metal Fighter that you can customize. Battle Mode can be played locally with four players, or online with eight players. Each game involves three randomly selected rounds, and each of those only lasts a minute!

FAST FACT

When Sega created Sonic, they came up with other ideas for the character, including an armadillo, a dog, a rabbit, and an old man with a mustache—who they used as the design for Eggman instead!

Scrap metal

Zap Scrap is a bit like playing laser tag—players shoot at each other and earn points by scoring hits. If you take damage, your points go down. Power-up bullets can be found in item boxes, and it's a good idea to focus on getting these and dealing easy damage.

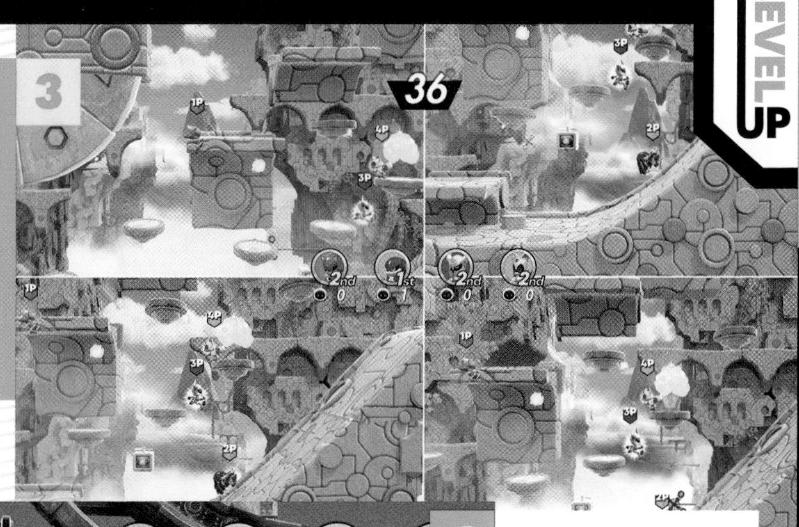

Star role

Star Snatcher gives you a time limit to collect stars: taking damage means you lose a star. There's also the *Fall Guys*–style Survival, where you have to avoid cannonballs and stay on the scaffolding—if you stand still for too long, the scaffolding will collapse. Falling off the screen eliminates you!

Get more metal drip

By playing the game online you can earn currency to buy more custom parts. However, they don't affect your performance—they just look cool. Overall this mode feels like something that could be developed more in the future—it could use more types of minigames to give it variety.

Sonic boom!

Shortly after the release of *Superstars* came *Sonic Dream Team*, a new 3D game for Apple platforms. It's pretty short, but some rate it as the best 3D *Sonic* in a long time!

TOP 10 MOBILE GAMES

Gaming on the move has never been more fun!

■ Mobile gaming offers a huge range of experiences, from simple two-minute puzzles to in-depth story-based games with hours of play in them—and we've picked a bit of everything for this top ten, so read on and find your next mobile fix!

10 Mech Arena

■ A game where you can send robots to battle each other is cool enough, but *Mech Arena* makes it even cooler by giving you a wide choice of mechs and many ways to customize them. You equip each one with two weapons, so the combo you choose makes a big difference to how your mech plays. Try out all the options, and then get good at your favorites!

AVAILABLE ON: PC, Mac, iOS, Android

09 Marvel Snap

■ There are plenty of card-collecting games out there, and Marvel is a big enough name that they could probably have gotten away with theirs being just OK. But with Ben Brode, one of the creators of *Hearthstone*, on board, they've made something that goes the extra mile. It's got a nice combination of simplicity and depth—games are short and based around capturing three locations, but as you learn the characters and different location types, you'll find each game plays out differently!

AVAILABLE ON: PC, Mac, iOS, Android

08 Forge of Empires

■ This is a god game where you have to develop a civilization from the Stone Age, build them a city to live in, and evolve their technology—and also come up with strategy for conflicts with other territories using turn-based combat. There are twenty-one different eras to progress through, and eventually you can colonize the solar system!

AVAILABLE ON:
PC, Mac, iOS, Android

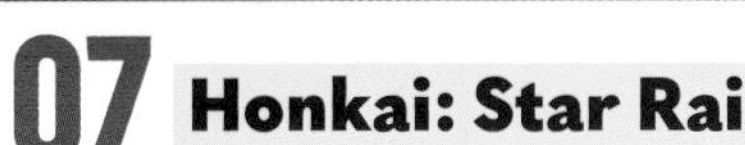

07 Honkai: Star Rail

■ Made by the studio that brought us *Genshin Impact*, and set in the same universe as their earlier game *Honkai Impact*, this is an RPG that uses turn-based combat, which is easier to manage on mobile devices (the game is available on other platforms, however). It's got a cool setup—you travel between planets on a space train—and the characters and story are engaging. And as with *Genshin Impact*, it's free to play—just don't get tempted into spending on gacha!

AVAILABLE ON: PS5, PC, iOS, Android

06 Slay the Spire

■ This combines dungeon-crawling games with card-collecting ones, and while it uses elements of *Warcraft* and *Magic: The Gathering* type games, it's actually really different from those. You win via combat random cards, which you add to your basic deck. A full run through the dungeon doesn't take that long, but you can go again and again, getting new cards and improving your game!

AVAILABLE ON: Nintendo Switch, PS4, Xbox One, PC, Mac, iOS, Android

05 Bombergrounds: Battle Royale

■ Yep, it's a *Bomberman* clone—but it's an excellent one. You play battle royale matches against other humans, you can drop bombs around the map, and you're equipped with a baseball bat to whack bombs away. In a neat twist, you also become larger when you collect stars—which makes you more powerful, but also slower. It's perfect when you want an MMO that's super quick to play—most matches only last a couple of minutes.

AVAILABLE ON: PC, Mac, iOS

04 TheoTown

■ There are a few *SimCity* clones available for mobile devices, but *TheoTown* is free (though you can buy in-game currency to acquire stuff for your city more quickly) and it does a very good impression of *SimCity 2000*, one of the best games in the series. There are few things more addictive than a good city-management game, and this one will have you going, "I'll just do one more thing before I stop," and then looking up and realizing an hour has passed.

AVAILABLE ON: PC, Mac, iOS, Android

03 Monument Valley

■ Puzzle games work particularly well on mobile devices, which is why there are tons of them—but *Monument Valley* stands out for its beautiful design and clever puzzles, which use optical illusions and impossible shapes. It might not be the most challenging game, but it's great to play when you're feeling stressed out—which means it's very good to have on your phone!

AVAILABLE ON: PC, iOS, Android

02 Hearthstone

■ This mobile spin-off of the *World of Warcraft* card game is free-to-play, making it a great way for newcomers to experience *Warcraft*. You just hop on and the game will randomly pit you against another player. It's turn-based and the developers have worked to make it fast and fun—though like the full game, buying cards with real money will strengthen your hand and help you win, so if you do get into *Hearthstone*, be careful not to spend too much on it!

AVAILABLE ON: PC, Mac, iOS, Android

01 Pokémon GO

■ *Pokémon GO* launched in 2016 and at first everyone seemed to be playing it. It soon calmed down (and news sites moved on from running stories about people having accidents or being a nuisance while playing the game), but it's still going strong because it's just a really good take on Pokémon. Being able to catch your own Pokémon while out walking never gets old (even if it's easier to catch them if you turn AR off), especially when new Pokémon keep being added to the game. Events and new types of battle keep it fresh!

AVAILABLE ON: iOS, Android

DAYS OF DOOM

POST-APOCALYPSE, BUT MAKE IT CUTE.

This appealingly cartoony turn-based RPG is set in the midst of a zombie apocalypse. It was originally developed for mobile devices, but legendary games producer Atari stepped in to help them bring it to consoles and Steam.

The premise is simple: you're a group of survivors, you've heard there's a safe place called Sanctuary, and you're traveling through a procedurally generated map in the hope of reaching it. Getting there will cost gas, and there'll be fights along the way and stuff to collect that you can level up with. Experienced players of this kind of game may find it a little too easy and short, but it's a good one for newcomers—and whichever you are, it's a fun ride.

QUICK TIPS

TAKE AIM

■ Look out for healers in the ranks of enemy parties—target them first to stop them undoing all the damage you inflict by healing the rest.

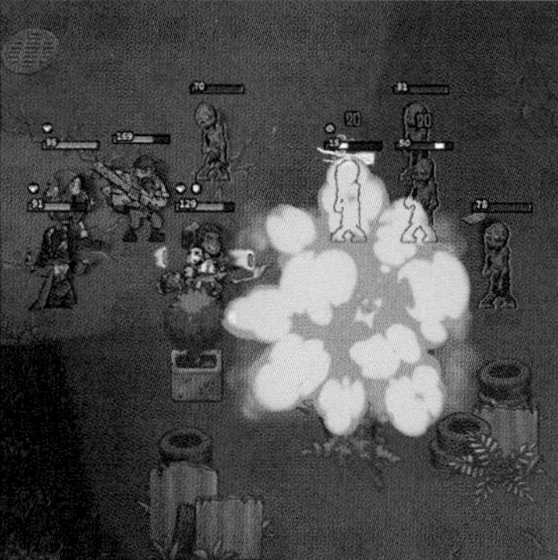

REPEAT OFFENDER

■ Pay attention to characters' buffs and debuffs, as you can get additional and longer-lasting effects during combat, such as damage that continues for more than one turn.

WATCH OUT!

■ Upgrading the Watchtower and Town Hall at your settlement have useful benefits, so don't ignore them. The Watchtower allows you to increase the limit of heroes you can keep.

RUNDOWN OF A RUN

Your team makes a series of runs in their efforts to get to Sanctuary, and the run is over if you run out of gas or everyone dies. Here's what you can expect to encounter…

MAKE THE TEAM WORK

At the start of each run, you put together a squad of three to venture out. Getting a good mix of skills is essential, and you can unlock more survivors as you go along.

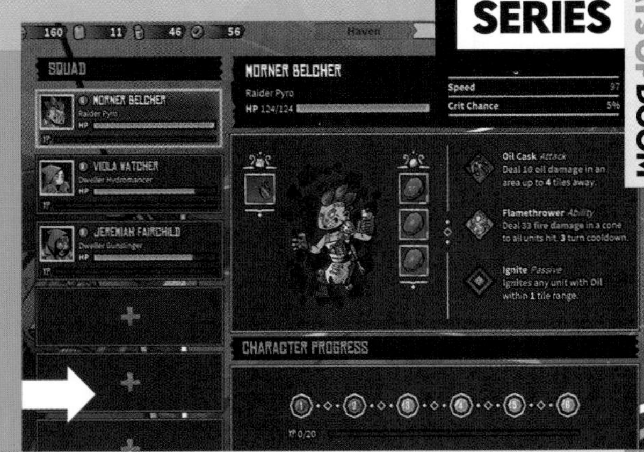

RUNE FOR IMPROVEMENT

You can also acquire Runes and then equip them to your characters, boosting particular scores. Buying online isn't an option in the apocalypse, so it's useful there are still some shops around!

MAP IT OUT

There are some great touches in this game—like how when you bring up the map, it isn't just a thing that appears on the screen, but a thing the characters spread out on a table to read.

NEW MUTANTS

You're not just up against waves of zombies all the time—there are also large, shambling mutants to tackle. The hand-drawn artwork is superb, and really lifts the whole experience.

FAST FACT

Atari was the maker of *Pong*, one of the first home gaming consoles, and the Atari 2600, a console which was launched in 1977 and stayed in shops until 1992!

LIKE THIS? TRY THIS:

SLAY THE SPIRE

This game is part of the reason why there are so many roguelike games with turn-based combat these days. Its card-collecting system for combat adds an addictive edge to its dungeon-crawling action!

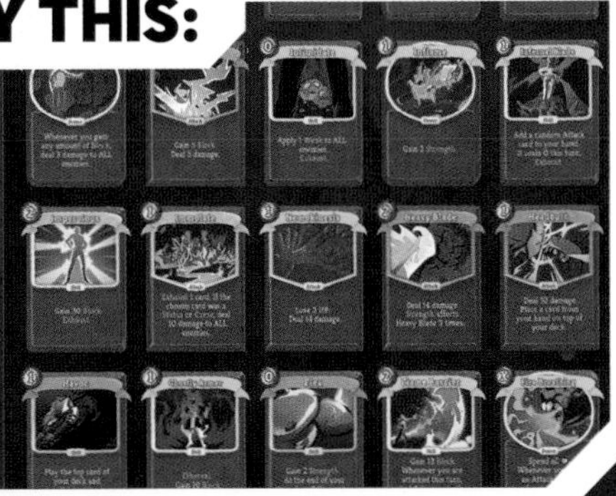

DreamWorks All-Star Kart Racing

Teamwork makes the DreamWorks!

■ You wait years for a *Mario Kart* clone based around characters from a major animation studio and then two come along at once. Following hot on the heels of *Disney Speedstorm*, *DreamWorks All-Star Kart Racing* differs in one important way—it's not free-to-play. So it's more expensive up front, but it means you don't have in-game purchases nagging at you.

The DreamWorks roster isn't quite as appealing as Disney's: they're the studio that made *Shrek*, *Madagascar*, *How to Train Your Dragon*, *Boss Baby*, *Trolls*, and *Kung Fu Panda*. But whether they're favorite characters of yours or not, it's the racing that counts...

Not their first rodeo

■ This isn't the first game to have this exact premise—*DreamWorks Super Star Kartz* in 2011 matched this stable of characters with this particular sport. Amazingly, despite his huge popularity this is the first video game to feature Shrek since then.

You can handle this

As with *Speedstorm*, this game sticks to the *Mario Kart* template and captures the overall feel of its more successful rival. The karts handle in a very similar way, there's a drifting mechanism, and you pick up power-ups and weapons.

Underpower-ups

The items aren't as game-changing as the ones in *Mario Kart*, but this puts the focus more firmly on the actual racing. It also means that *Mario Kart*'s habit of giving great items to racers at the back and weak ones to those at the front isn't an issue here!

Dirt tracks

In some ways this is more challenging than other kart racing games—you'll find the patches of mud on the track completely kill your drift, and you need to adjust pretty quick when this happens. And at higher speed settings, the opposition AIs can get really aggressive.

FAST FACT

The studio that made this, Bamtang Games, is responsible for another series of cartoon kart racers, the *Nickelodeon Kart Racers* games. Avoid the first game in the series, but the second and third are pretty good.

No need to switch

Switch gamers won't find much in this game to divert them from *Mario Kart*, but PlayStation and Xbox users keen for an alternative on their platform—one where they're not constantly being nudged to spend extra money to unlock stuff—should check it out!

KIRBY'S RETURN TO DREAM LAND DELUXE

A CLASSIC *KIRBY* OUTING REMASTERED FOR THE SWITCH!

Kirby has been riding high after *Kirby and the Forgotten Land* became the first Kirby game to outsell the original *Kirby's Dream Land*, which came out on the Game Boy back in 1992! So this Switch remaster of *Kirby's Return to Dream Land* arrives at the perfect time.

Return to Dream Land was made for the Wii, and was hailed as one of the best in the series when it came out in 2011. Whereas *The Forgotten Land* brought Kirby into a fully 3D world, this is a reminder of how great the character still is in classic *Kirby* platform action! Up to four players can work together to complete the main story, or compete against each other in minigames!

QUICK TIPS

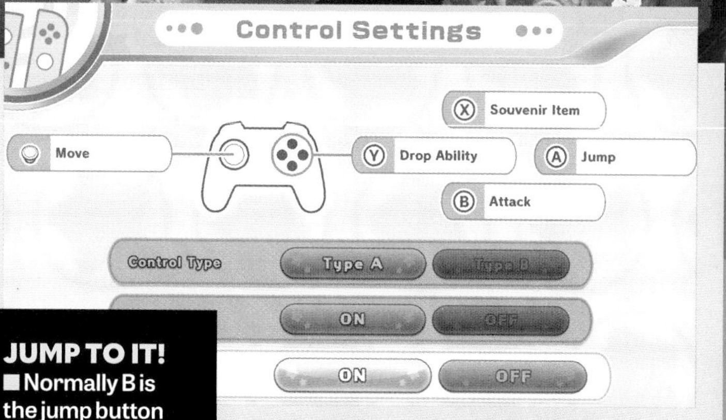

Control Settings

Souvenir Item
Move
Drop Ability
Jump
Attack
Control Type
Type A
Type B
ON
OFF
ON
OFF

JUMP TO IT!

■ Normally B is the jump button on Switch games, but weirdly in this game it isn't. You can change to a different controller layout, which makes B jump and Y attack, and we recommend it!

TIME FOR SCHOOL

■ Kirby's Copy Abilities all have a set of moves to learn—but you don't have to do it by trial and error. Just pause and go into the menu—all the moves are listed there!

COPYCAT

■ Sometimes you need a particular Copy Ability but there's no enemy in the area with the right one. Make a note of it and come back when you do have the right ability equipped.

CRASHING IN

■ The plot opens with a spaceship crashing on the planet Popstar, piloted by a traveler named Magalor. Kirby is tasked with finding the five pieces of the ship . . .

GRAB A COPY

■ In the usual *Kirby* style, you can swallow different enemies and copy their abilities. There are twenty-six different Copy Abilities in *Deluxe*, five of which also appear as amped-up super-abilities!

HACK AND SLASH

■ Sword is the best-known of Kirby's Copy Abilities, and one you'll end up using a fair bit. (We like how you get a Link-style hat as well as the sword.) But there are better Copy Abilities in *Deluxe* . . .

NINJA SKILLS

■ Ninja makes you faster, lets you hang from walls, and throw needles. Fighter gives you *Street Fighter*–style martial arts attacks. Bomb is simple but very effective—you can produce and throw bombs!

MECHA MOVE

■ Two new Copy Abilities have been created just for *Deluxe*—Sand gives Kirby sand-based powers, but Mecha is the best ability in the game, granting robot armor, which comes with a jet pack and lots of cool attacks!

FAST FACT

US lawyer John Kirby defended Nintendo when a studio claimed *Donkey Kong* was a rip-off of their movie *King Kong*. He won, and Nintendo named a cute balloon guy after him to say thanks!

LIKE THIS? TRY THIS:

KIRBY STAR ALLIES

■ Kirby's debut adventure on the Switch is very much in the same style as *Return to Dream Land*—it doesn't do much that's new, but if you're looking for more of the same, look no further.

MERRY MINIGAMES

Small is definitely beautiful with the Kirby minigames!

Clearing the second stage of Cookie Country unlocks one of *Deluxe*'s new game modes: Merry Magoland, a theme park featuring eleven minigames for local multiplayer fun. The minigames mostly come from previous Kirby adventures, but three new ones have been created just for *Deluxe*. And you can earn character masks you can wear in the main game!

1 Check please

■ Taken from *Kirby: Squeak Squad*, "Smash Ride" sees players trying to knock each other out of an arena using Smash Stars. Staying in the arena is also the objective in "Checkerboard Chase," from *Kirby 64: The Crystal Shards*—in this, players try to make squares on the checkerboard fall, in the hope of making opponents fall with them.

2 Dojo mojo

■ "Ninja Dojo" was in the original version of *Return to Dream Land*, and sees you competing to hit targets with shuriken (ninja throwing stars). "Kirby on the Draw," from *Kirby Super Star Ultra*, is another target-based game, this one with a Wild West theme.

3

Maximum volume

■ "Magolor's Tome Trackers" is one of the new games created for *Deluxe*—in this you have to race to identify and locate the book Magolor is thinking of. Also new for *Deluxe* is "Booming Blasters," where players run around an arena trying to shoot each other with lasers. Wholesome!

4

The first cut

■ As well as "Samurai Kirby," which comes from *Kirby Super Star* and challenges you to get in with the quickest strike on your opponents, there's "Samurai Kirby 100," a new online single-player version where you compete against the times of ninety-nine other players from around the world!

Starring role

■ Between 2001 and 2003, Kirby starred in his own anime series, titled *Kirby of the Stars* in Japan and *Kirby: Right Back at Ya!* for English-speaking audiences. It ran for one hundred episodes and saw Kirby battling monsters supplied to villains by NightMare Enterprises.

5

It's not over

■ Finish the main game and you can unlock "Magolor Epilogue"—an extra campaign where you play as Magolor! He's stranded in another dimension and has lost most of his magic powers. This extends the play time of the game by another couple of hours. And if you gain a gold ranking on every stage and boss battle, you can unlock a further secret stage!

GLOOMHAVEN

A REAL CHALLENGE FOR RPG FIENDS!

The *Gloomhaven* tabletop game started life as a Kickstarter in 2015 and has since become a modern classic. Like a lot of recent board games, it can be tricky to pick up—but its co-op dungeon-crawling campaigns and card-based action are perfectly designed when you get the hang of them. So it's no surprise a video game followed, first on PC and Mac in 2021, before coming to consoles in 2023.

It's very faithful to the tabletop game, using a hexagonal gameplay area. Thankfully it has a detailed tutorial to help you learn how to play—but even when you do, it's a tough game to beat! It's recommended for players who are already familiar with turn-based RPGs looking for a new challenge.

QUICK TIPS

GIVE IT A REST

■ Long or short rests both cost one discarded card, so a long rest is better value, but make sure you're not at risk of dropping below 1 HP, as this leaves you vulnerable.

MAKE IT PERSONAL

■ Check each character's personal quests and keep those objectives in mind as you play—there are rewards for fulfilling these.

ON THE BACK BURNER

■ You can burn cards to gain more powerful attacks, but at the next rest you lose two cards, meaning you'll be exhausted more quickly! If you have to do it, save it for later in the battle.

IT'S ON THE CARDS

The Campaign mode is a straight version of the tabletop game, including all ninety-five missions. But there's another mode, Guildmaster, which is more tailored to the video game experience. New players are advised to play Guildmaster first, because that's where the tutorial is! But let's break down the basics for you.

STRIKE AND MOVE

In each round of a battle, you draw two cards for each member of the party. You then choose a top action (usually attack) and a bottom action (usually movement).

REUSE OR REFUSE

Some cards are temporarily discarded after being played and come back into your deck after a rest. But the more powerful actions, with an icon in the bottom right corner, can only be used once.

OUT OF OPTIONS

The top action comes first, then the bottom action. If a character no longer has two cards to play, that means they're exhausted and drop out of the fight!

LOOT'S GREAT

As you level up, the enemies you face also improve, so make sure you loot so you can get better gear! Donate your loot to the Sanctuary of the Great Oak and get the rewards for raising your prosperity level.

FAST FACT

The Guildmaster version of the game has a different progression system and 160 missions, including new locations not visited in the original game. There's also a sandbox version, where all characters are unlocked.

LIKE THIS? TRY THIS:

MARVEL'S MIDNIGHT SUNS

This deck-building RPG was a surprising flop when it came out in 2022, and a planned Switch release was canceled, but it's worth another look. The central idea, that you play a new superhero you can customize with different powers, is really cool!

GLOOMHAVEN PARTY GUIDE

Get the right mix of characters!

The characters you need for a balanced party will be different depending on how large the party is, which means character classes aren't always great or always weak. All characters are good in a party of four, where there are others to balance them out, but some are better than others.

1

The top starters

The best starting characters are Mindthief and Red Guard—these two both work very well in all sizes of party, though Red Guard is easier to use for new players. Of the unlockable characters, Berserker and Plagueherald can be used in any party. Beast Tyrant, Doomstalker, Sawbones, and Sunkeeper are good for a party of three.

2

The all-arounders

Nightshade and Quartermaster are great in all parties, but you won't have those available from the start. From the starting characters, Brute and Spellweaver are good all-arounders and work in any party, but you'll unlock better characters later, which will make them redundant.

FAST FACT

The tabletop version of *Gloomhaven* topped the all-time greatest games chart on the BoardGameGeek website for more than five years!

3

Good in a duo

■ In a party of two, the best ones to go for from the starting characters are Cragheart, Mindthief, and Red Guard—and of these, Cragheart is the most useful and flexible. The unlockables that work well in a two-person party—apart from Nightshade and Quartermaster—are Beast Tyrant, Berserker, and Plagueherald.

4

Best in a gang

■ Scoundrel, Hatchet, and Voidwarden come into their own in parties of four, but are better avoided in parties of two. Similarly, Soothsinger is pretty mid in a party of two, but in parties of three and four is a top-tier character—one of the best support characters in the game.

Turn around

■ The sequence of combat is incredibly important—don't move toward enemies without taking into account how many of them have a turn after yours, as you don't want to get surrounded. You can also sometimes force them to waste turns by moving toward you!

5

Steer clear

■ The weakest characters overall are Summoner, Elementalist, Demolitionist, Diviner, and Tinkerer. Diviner, Tinkerer, and Voidwarden have significant weaknesses that mean you should avoid them completely in parties of two unless you want a real challenge!

DESTINY 2: THE FINAL SHAPE

The epic series arrives at its destination!

The free-to-play FPS *Destiny 2* launched back in 2017, going deeper into the mythic SF world established by the original *Destiny*. It's received several pay-to-play expansions since then, each with their own seasons. *The Final Shape* was originally scheduled for February 2024, but was delayed to make it "bigger and bolder" and developer Bungie says it's "the culmination of the first ten years of Destiny storytelling," featuring the climax of the Light and Darkness saga that began in the very first game…

BEARING WITNESS

■ *The Final Shape* sees the player chasing and confronting the Witness, *Destiny*'s chief villain, and preventing them from creating the Final Shape that will destroy all life in the universe. So, no pressure.

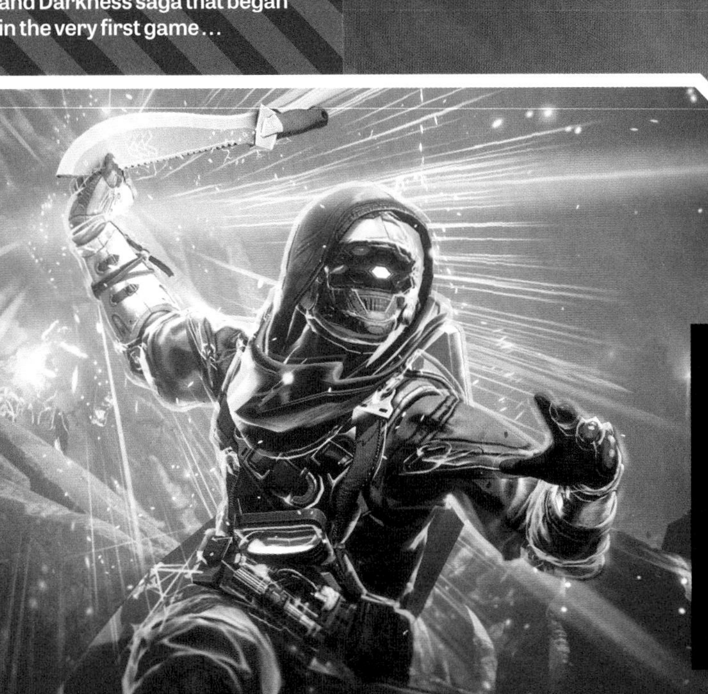

GET THE EDGE

■ All the classes receive a new Super Ability in this expansion. Arc Hunters have Storm's Edge, which is described like this: "Dagger in hand, become the Arc flashing in the darkness; the edge of the storm your enemies cannot outrun."

LEARN A NEW SONG

■ Solar Warlocks get Song of Flame: "Unleash your inner phoenix with every attack. Buff your weapons, allies, and harness the living Solar flame." Void Titans have Twilight Arsenal: "Blades honed by the Void cut through the air. Lift them from the feet of your felled foes and continue the attack."

THE NEXT EPISODE

■ It's been confirmed *Destiny* will continue after *The Final Shape* with a new storyline, but it's going to shift away from seasonal updates and move to a new system of releasing episodes. We'll have to wait and see what form that takes . . .

HEART OF THE COUNTRY

■ It takes place in a new region, Pale Heart, "a place of new wonders and old memories" that has already been affected by the Witness's actions—and that is inhabited by the Subjugators, enforcers working for the Witness, who possess Strand and Stasis powers.

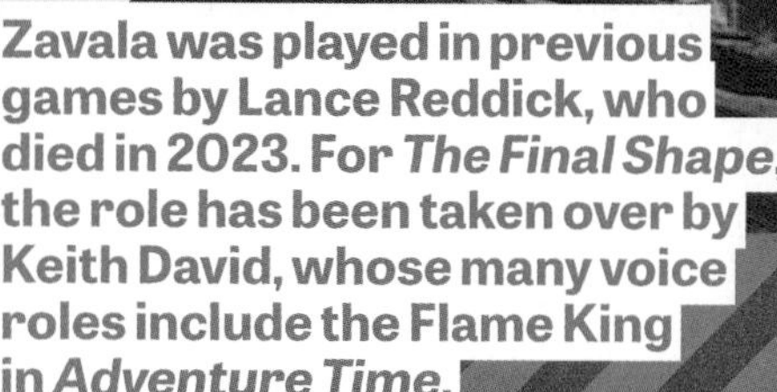

FAST FACT

Zavala was played in previous games by Lance Reddick, who died in 2023. For *The Final Shape*, the role has been taken over by Keith David, whose many voice roles include the Flame King in *Adventure Time*.

MINECRAFT LEGENDS

THIS ISN'T JUST SURVIVAL—IT'S WAR!

Minecraft is still comfortably the best-selling game of all time, and is being refreshed with regular updates, so there's really no need for a *Minecraft 2*. Instead, the future of *Minecraft* seems to be games that use its familiar and flexible world to do new things.

Minecraft Legends is a strategy game where you command your army to defeat the forces of evil. Strategy games can be very complicated, but the *Minecraft* version simplifies the genre and seeks to open it up to a new audience. In this case, the Overworld is being invaded by Piglins from the Nether, and it's your job to drive them back. It's light on story and heavy on Piglins!

QUICK TIPS

REMEMBER TO SPECIALIZE

■ Your army should have a mix of types, and you should make use of their strengths. For instance, use Stone Golems against structures, while deploying Creepers and Skeletons to tackle hostile mobs.

WALLS AND TRAPS

■ Always fortify each village you come to with defensive walls and watchtowers. And you can use that *Minecraft* creativity to build traps for them!

KEEP IT COMING

■ Because building fortifications is so important, you should max out your resources at every opportunity—you'll need them! Always set some harvesting in motion when you arrive at a new village.

LEADING THE TROOPS

Strategy games aren't just about planning attacks—they're also about how you manage your resources. This is where real wars are won and lost, and it fits in perfectly with *Minecraft*, which is based around gathering resources.

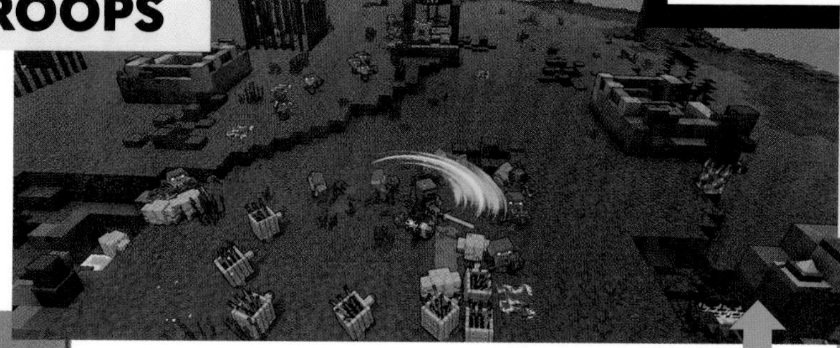

ALLAYS AND ALLIES

The Build Allays and Gather Allays do the key tasks for you, freeing you to concentrate on war. Fighting is done by Creepers, Skeletons, Warriors, Zombies, and Golems. The regular Golem types are Cobblestone, Grindstone, Mossy, and Plank.

IN THE THICK OF IT

In a lot of strategy games, you're distanced from the action—a supreme commander ordering the troops from a position of safety. But *Minecraft Legends* puts you on the battlefield with different types of allies.

DIFFERENT EVERY TIME

Just like in regular Minecraft, the world is procedurally generated at the start of each new game, so each game takes place in a unique world—and the tar pools will be in a different place each time!

GET IN FIRST

There are four "First" Golems—First of Brick, First of Diorite, First of Oak, and First of Stone. The Firsts can only be found in tar pools, which you must search the map to find.

FAST FACT

The long, long, long-awaited *Minecraft* live-action movie is set to release in 2025, with Jack Black as Steve!

LIKE THIS? TRY THIS:

STARCRAFT

If *Minecraft Legends* has whetted your appetite for strategy games, you can get *Starcraft*—one of the most important video games in history—as a free download. It pits humans, aliens, and robots against each other in a battle for resources!

THE LONGEST RUNNING GAME SERIES . . . EVER!

Join us for a trip back through gaming history to find the series that have been around the longest . . .

STREET FIGHTER

FIRST GAME: *Street Fighter*, August 1987

LATEST GAME: *Street Fighter 6*, June 2023

TIME BETWEEN: 35 years

■ The original *Street Fighter* was decent, but the sequel became the hottest arcade game around by including a selection of eight playable fighters, each with their own special moves. It still leads the field in fighting games today!

FINAL FANTASY

FIRST GAME: *Final Fantasy*, December 1987

LATEST GAME: *Final Fantasy VII Rebirth*, 2024

TIME BETWEEN: 36 years

■ *Final Fantasy* has produced sixteen main-series games and many spin-offs and remakes, which makes the title a bit ironic really—but this is one of the great RPG series, which always tries to do new things with each installment.

DOUBLE DRAGON

FIRST GAME: *Double Dragon*, April 1987

LATEST GAME: *Double Dragon Gaiden: Rise of the Dragons*, July 2023

TIME BETWEEN: 36 years

■ This was the original beat-'em-up—you stride along punching goons and confronting bosses. Its success in arcades made it a big enough name that there's always interest in a new version. Recent games have gone down a retro route.

BUBBLE BOBBLE

FIRST GAME: *Bubble Bobble*, August 1986

LATEST GAME: *Puzzle Bobble Everybubble!*, May 2023

TIME BETWEEN: 36 years

■ This cute and ingenious arcade game, in which you play as dinosaurs clearing screens of enemies by trapping them in bubbles and popping them, was ported to almost every platform in the 1980s and 1990s—and morphed into the equally popular *Puzzle Bobble*!

METROID

FIRST GAME: *Metroid*, August 1986

LATEST GAME: *Metroid Prime Remastered*, February 2023

TIME BETWEEN: 36 years

■ For this sci-fi action platformer, Nintendo combined elements of two other game series: *Mario* and *Zelda*. *Metroid Prime* on the GameCube saw a move to 3D and is possibly the best in the series, but 2021's *Metroid Dread* went back to 2D and is the biggest-selling *Metroid* game!

THE LEGEND OF ZELDA

FIRST GAME: *The Legend of Zelda*, February 1986

LATEST GAME: *The Legend of Zelda: Tears of the Kingdom*, May 2023

TIME BETWEEN: 37 years

■ Few game series can come close to *The Legend of Zelda* in terms of quality—many of them having a strong claim on being the best game of all time. It's one of the pillars of Nintendo, and it's hard to imagine it ever ending!

DRAGON QUEST

FIRST GAME: *Dragon Quest*, May 1986

LATEST GAME: *Dragon Quest Monsters: The Dark Prince*, December 2023

TIME BETWEEN: 37 years

■ One of the big-hitters of Japanese RPGs, *Dragon Quest* had great storytelling and made the genre easier for newcomers to pick up. It's spawned eleven games in its main series, but also spin-off series, novels, manga, and anime.

Q*BERT

FIRST GAME: *Q*bert*, October 1982

LATEST GAME: *Q*bert*, October 2019

TIME BETWEEN: 37 years

■ This arcade game was unusual for its sort-of-3D angle on the action—which is why its main character is called Q*bert—it sounds like "cube." Its puzzle elements still work well on mobile devices today!

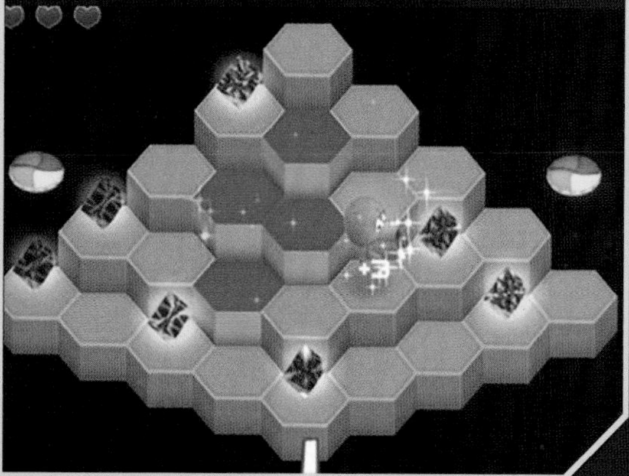

BURGERTIME

FIRST GAME: *BurgerTime*, August 1982

LATEST GAME: *BurgerTime Party!*, October 2019

TIME BETWEEN: 37 years

■ This burger-themed arcade game, in which chef Peter Pepper must collect hamburger ingredients while dodging the foodstuffs chasing him, has had a surprising afterlife, and sequels have regularly appeared ever since. People love burgers, we guess!

DRAGON SLAYER

FIRST GAME: *Dragon Slayer*, September 1984

LATEST GAME: *The Legend of Heroes: Trails Through Daybreak II*, September 2022

TIME BETWEEN: 38 years

■ *Dragon Slayer* took the RPG genre and replaced its turn-based combat with hack-and-slash action. It's remained a huge franchise in Japan, with over fifty games across multiple spin-off series including *Xanadu*, *Sorcerian*, *Lord Monarch*, and *The Legend of Heroes*.

NOBUNAGA'S AMBITION

FIRST GAME: *Nobunaga no Yabō*, March 1983

LATEST GAME: *Nobunaga's Ambition: Awakening*, July 2022

TIME BETWEEN: 39 years

■ One of the first turn-based strategy RPGs, the goal of *Nobunaga* games is to conquer and unify feudal Japan. The series's huge popularity in Japan has kept it running, but strategy game fans worldwide reckon these are among the finest ever made!

BOMBERMAN

FIRST GAME: *Bomber Man*, July 1983

LATEST GAME: *Super Bomberman R 2*, September 2023

TIME BETWEEN: 40 years

■ Initially released on home computers, *Bomberman* became a hit on the NES—and has stayed popular because it's such a great multi-player game. It's come back strongly with the *R* games in recent years!

FROGGER

FIRST GAME: *Frogger*, August 1981

LATEST GAME: *Frogger and the Rumbling Ruins*, 2022

TIME BETWEEN: 41 years

■ You've played *Crossy Road*? This is where they got the idea. Guide frogs through traffic and across a river: that's it. But it's insanely addictive, and it's been reinvented again and again!

MICROSOFT FLIGHT SIMULATOR

FIRST GAME: *Microsoft Flight Simulator*, November 1982

LATEST GAME: *Microsoft Flight Simulator 2024*, 2024

TIME BETWEEN: 42 years

■ Microsoft's earliest software was mostly business-based, but they wanted something that would show the power of the latest PCs and came up with this. It is Microsoft's longest-running software line—it's three years older than Windows!

MISSILE COMMAND

FIRST GAME: *Missile Command*, July 1980

LATEST GAME: *Missile Command: Recharged*, November 2022

TIME BETWEEN: 42 years

■ One of the most stressful games of the golden age of arcades, *Missile Command* saw you protecting cities by destroying the missiles being dropped on them. That terrifying Cold War experience has been made available for new generations of gamers ever since.

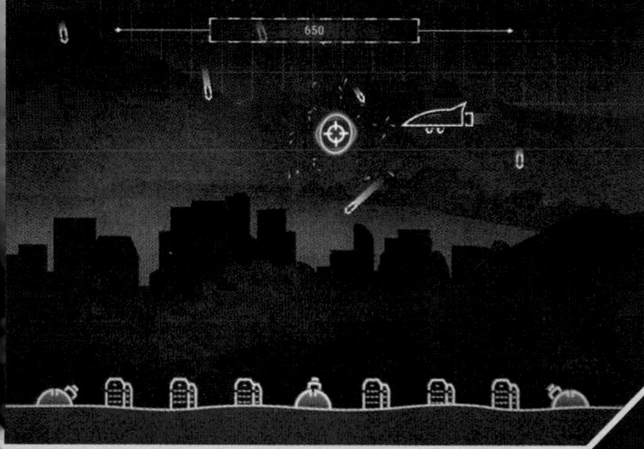

MARIO

FIRST GAME: *Donkey Kong*, July 1981

LATEST GAME: *Mario vs. Donkey Kong*, February 2024

TIME BETWEEN: 42 years

■ The little guy that launched a company. Mario didn't even have a name when he appeared in *Donkey Kong*—he was just called Jumpman—but he's since appeared in multiple games on every Nintendo platform, and the *Mario* series is easily the biggest-selling of all time!

ASTEROIDS

FIRST GAME: *Asteroids*, 1979

LATEST GAME: *Asteroids: Recharged*, December 2021

TIME BETWEEN: 42 years

■ Atari's attempt at a *Space Invaders* type game didn't take off in Japan, but was huge in America and keeps coming back on new platforms. *Asteroids: Recharged* adds new power-ups to the classic gameplay!

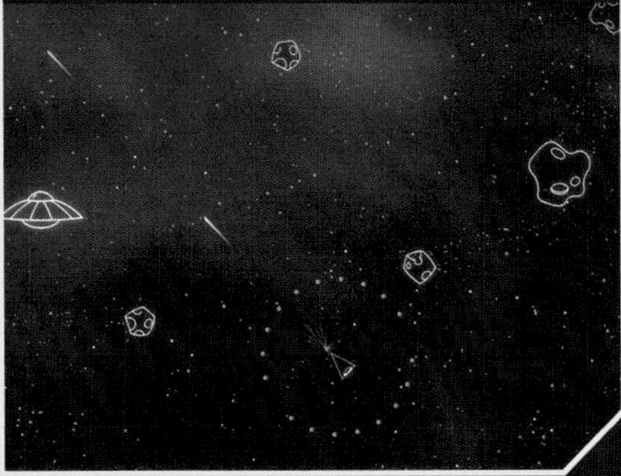

WIZARDRY

FIRST GAME: *Wizardry: Proving Grounds of the Mad Overlord*, September 1981

LATEST GAME: *Wizardry: Proving Grounds of the Mad Overlord* (3D remake), September 2023

TIME BETWEEN: 42 years

■ The granddaddy of RPGs, *Wizardry* came out as *Dungeons & Dragons* was becoming popular. It was designed in America but became huge in Japan, where dozens of spin-offs from the main range have been created. This is where the Japanese love of sword-and-sorcery RPGs comes from!

GALAXIAN

FIRST GAME: *Galaxian*, September 1979

LATEST GAME: *Galaga Wars+*, November 2021

TIME BETWEEN: 42 years

■ *Galaxian* was designed to compete with *Space Invaders* and was one of the first games with color graphics. The sequel, *Galaga*, was even more popular—and the series turned out to be perfectly suited to gaming on mobile devices!

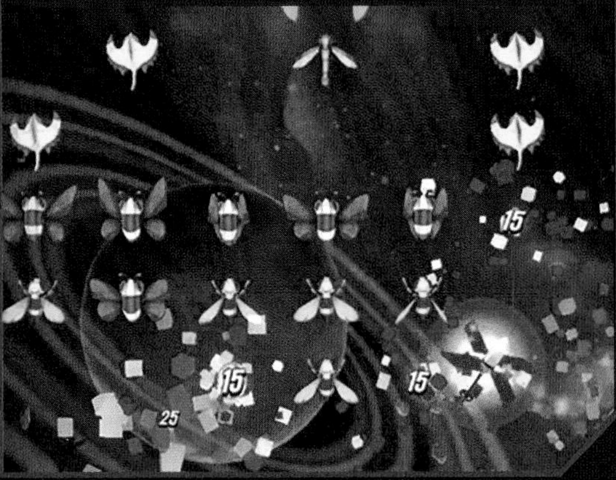

PAC-MAN

FIRST GAME: *Pac-Man*, July 1980

LATEST GAME: *Pac-Man World Re-Pac*, August 2022

TIME BETWEEN: 44 years

■ One of the most recognizable characters in gaming, *Pac-Man* shot to fame in the maze chase arcade game, but he's since appeared in many genres. Surely it's time to bring back the Switch battle royale game *Pac-Man 99*!

SPACE INVADERS

FIRST GAME: *Space Invaders*, June 1978

LATEST GAME: *Space Invaders: World Defense*, July 2023

TIME BETWEEN: 45 years

■ *Space Invaders* kickstarted video games as we know them today. A simple shooting game, it quickly became more popular than any arcade game had ever been. Since then, it's come out on various Atari consoles, the NES, the Game Boy, the PlayStation, phones, watches, and calculators. The latest version on Android, *World Defense*, uses AR technology. It's simple but unstoppable!

PONG

FIRST GAME: *Pong*, November 1972

LATEST GAME: *Pong Quest*, May 2020

TIME BETWEEN: 47 years

■ Back in the 1970s, this tennis game was video gaming excitement! It was adapted for different sports, and there was a home console version that ONLY played *Pong*, but the most recent game, *Pong Quest*, is a dungeon-crawling RPG—somehow?!

THE OREGON TRAIL

FIRST GAME: *The Oregon Trail*, December 1971

LATEST GAME: *The Oregon Trail* (Xbox version), August 2023

TIME BETWEEN: 51 years

■ The *Oregon Trail* began as a text-based game simulating life as a pioneer in the 19th century. Its first release was to an eighth-grade history class in Minnesota that was taught by Don Rawitsch, the game's creator. It later became available to more schools, and a more advanced version was made for the Apple II computer in 1985. Its sequels and spin-offs include *The Yukon Trail*, *The Amazon Trail*, *The Orion Trail* (a space version), and *The Organ Trail* (a zombie version). A full, updated remake is available for iOS, Windows, Switch, and Xbox—including playable Native American characters for the first time. It might be the most unlikely success story in gaming history!

SUPER BOMBERMAN R 2

IT IS, QUITE LITERALLY, THE BOMB!

The *Bomberman* series has come back in a big way! It was one of Nintendo's most popular games in the era of the NES and SNES, but *Super Bomberman R* was the first new *Bomberman* game in years, and its multiplayer action captured a whole new audience.

The gameplay in this sequel is much the same: you travel through a grid filled with obstacles and enemies and use bombs to break the obstacles and take out enemies—while making sure you don't get caught in your own blast. The aim is to be the last survivor. It's at its best in couch-based multiplayer: it's so much more satisfying to blow your friends up when they're sitting next to you!

QUICK TIPS

BOOM!
■ *Bomberman* is like a puzzle game where the board constantly changes. Everyone's bombs are always blowing up parts of the arena, so being aware of the state of the board is essential.

STAYING ALIVE
■ You don't get extra credit for eliminations—just for being the last one alive. So don't rush to bomb others—you can let them blow one another up.

RUN INTERFERENCE
■ Focus on picking up power-ups, because you may struggle in a one-on-one battle against someone with more. But if you can't reach a power-up, blow it up to stop an opponent getting it!

IT'S BETTER TO BOMB TOGETHER

There is a single-player campaign in *Super Bomberman R 2*, but it's best approached as training for multiplayer if you've never played *Bomberman* before. Experienced players will be itching to get into one of its many multiplayer modes.

THE BIG BANG

Missing the free-to-play *Super Bomberman R Online*, with its great Battle 64 mode? Well, you can find it here! This game puts you up against sixty-three other players online.

YOU WON'T BE BOARD

Groups of you play against one another on different boards, then some of you are told to quickly escape to another board to continue. Keep track of the exits on your board if you want to survive!

SET IT UP

This gets more interesting because the king chooses the board, and can build their own boards, Super Mario Maker–style! Though you do have to play a board before you can save it, so it can't be totally unplayable.

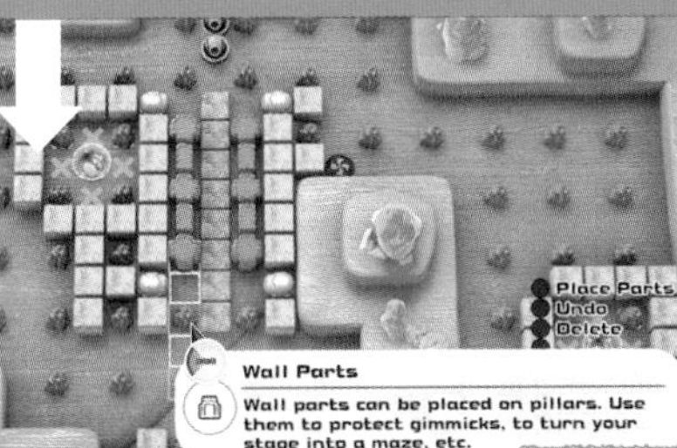

BATTLE ROYAL

There's also a new mode called Castle, where fifteen players team up against one player who's the "king"—and who has extra powers the others don't. The others must collect keys and unlock chests.

FAST FACT

There was a manga based on *Bomberman* in the late 1990s, which was adapted into an anime, which was then adapted into . . . a video game, *Bomberman B-Daman Bakugaiden: The Road to Victory*, on the Game Boy Color.

LIKE THIS? TRY THIS:

TINY TANKS

This *Roblox* game has a different look from most games on the platform, and it's an absolute gem—warfare between two armies of toy tanks in various household settings. Even if you don't usually like Roblox games, try it out!

GHOST TRICK: PHANTOM DETECTIVE

A GAME WITH A SURPRISING AFTERLIFE!

And my ghost tricks can only get me so far.

Minutes Before Death

You're a ghost. You've lost your memory. And you have to prevent a murder—which may help you to solve your own.

Ghost Trick: Phantom Detective is a puzzle game that originally came out for the DS back in 2010. It didn't sell well and was regarded as a flop—but over the years it found a lot of fans and became a cult classic. Now it's back with an HD remaster on all major platforms.

The game was created by Shu Takumi, the man responsible for the *Ace Attorney* series, and like those games it's wackily overdramatic and has a cast of weird characters. It's a really unique gaming experience, and the art and animation are quite special!

QUICK TIPS

EXPLORE DIFFERENT OPTIONS

■ Sometimes the solution is to stop the killer—but sometimes it's to put the victim out of harm's way.

CHECK THE RECORD

■ Like a lot of mystery games, *Ghost Trick* keeps a log of everything you've found out so far—and it's always worth checking it and reminding yourself of info you may have forgotten.

EAVESDROP

■ You can find out a lot of useful info by listening in on conversations—so look out for characters who are speaking on the phone, and remember you can travel down phone lines.

GETTING GHOSTED

Sissel, the player character, can travel four minutes into the past to prevent a detective called Lynne from getting shot. The problem is, her would-be assassins will try again—so Sissel will have to prevent it again.

THAT'S THE SPIRIT

Sissel can affect the world by possessing inanimate objects. The puzzle is how to use them to interfere with the course of events and prevent the murder. Pressing the "Ghost" button takes you into the ghost dimension, where time stops.

THE CLUES ARE THERE

The only objects you can affect are important to the puzzle—so it's about working out what you're meant to do with them, rather than searching the room for objects to manipulate.

GET A DO-OVER

Sissel can keep rewinding time, going back to the start of his four-minute window—so you can keep trying until you get everything to click and Lynne is saved.

WALK THE DOG

The game is divided into eighteen chapters, all taking place over a single night—and along the way you can find the clues to why Sissel was killed. Oh, and you can control the ghost of a dog in the later chapters. Did we mention this is a strange game?

FAST FACT

A limited edition of *Ghost Trick: Phantom Detective*, released in Japan, includes a board game designed by Shu Takumi called *Escape from the Toy Factory*. A deluxe edition also includes the soundtrack on CD and a set of playing cards.

LIKE THIS? TRY THIS:

PHOENIX WRIGHT: ACE ATTORNEY TRILOGY

The *Ace Attorney* courtroom-drama visual novels are some of the best games ever made for the Game Boy Advance and Nintendo DS, so getting them all in one package is a bargain!

TOP 10 NEW INDIE GAMES

Check out our favorite creative, offbeat gems!

■ The indie games field has been really strong lately, so picking a top ten from the recent crop was a real challenge. Read on—maybe one of your favorites has made it in, or maybe you'll find something totally new!

10 Tents and Trees

■ This weirdly addictive puzzle game is, like all weirdly addictive puzzle games, really simple—you just have to place tents into a grid. The tents can't touch each other and must be next to a tree. You're basically putting together a nice orderly campsite. But it gets tricky as the levels go up!

AVAILABLE ON: Nintendo Switch, PC, iOS, Android

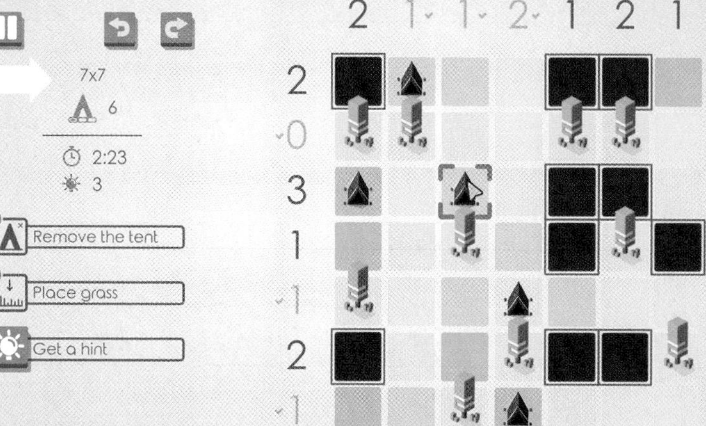

09 Planet of Lana

■ Big Studio Ghibli vibes from this Swedish-made puzzle-platform game, in which you control a teenage girl and her cat on a planet that's been invaded by robotic aliens. If you've played *Unravel* you'll have an idea of what to expect—it's not too challenging, but it looks great and the mysteries will keep you interested.

AVAILABLE ON: Nintendo Switch, PS5, PS4, Xbox Series S/X, Xbox One, PC

08 Venba

If any ignorant members of your family complain that video games are all violence and killing, prove them wrong with *Venba*, a totally wholesome and heartwarming experience. Venba is an Indian immigrant to Canada, and her mother's cookbook has been damaged. You must fill in the gaps and cook the recipes, while following Venba as she adapts to a new life in Toronto.

AVAILABLE ON:
Nintendo Switch, PS5, Xbox One, Xbox Series S/X, PC

07 Cocoon

Another puzzle adventure, this one sees you control a space beetle that can travel between worlds that are contained inside orbs. Yes, it's weird, but that's what indie games are for! It's a fairly short game but that's not always a bad thing, and the soundtrack is awesome. Stay chill when working on these puzzles, and let the solutions unfold in your mind!

AVAILABLE ON:
Nintendo Switch, PS5, PS4, Xbox Series S/X, Xbox One, PC

06 Viewfinder

In the future, all plant life on Earth has been wiped out, which sucks. But researchers are using a kind of VR world to investigate how they can be brought back. You move around that space, holding up photographs and drawings, and the things in the pictures become part of the world—so the puzzles are about finding where to place your pictures. Make sure to read all the notes if you want to get the whole story!

AVAILABLE ON: PS5, PS4, PC

05 Dredge

■ Fishing is the focus in this eerie horror game, in which you captain a fishing trawler around a series of islands and try to get a decent catch. But the islands are also full of mysteries—which you can learn more about by completing quests—and there are monsters in these waters. If you stay out on your boat at night, your panic meter rises and you may start to see things that aren't there!

AVAILABLE ON: Nintendo Switch, PS5, PS4, Xbox Series S/X, Xbox One, PC

04 Jack Jeanne

■ In this visual novel you play as Kisa, who is desperate to go to a top performing arts school... that only admits boys. Posing as a boy, she manages to get in—and from there the player has to organize her class schedule while also leaving social time. The game bursts into life with its rhythm games, as Kisa has to sing and dance. It's unusual to see theater in a video game, but it really works!

AVAILABLE ON: Nintendo Switch, iOS, Android

03 Pizza Tower

■ There's a feel of 1990s cartoons to this side-scrolling platform game, which is partly inspired by the *Wario Land* series. You play as Peppino Spaghetti, whose pizzeria is threatened with destruction when an intelligent pizza sets up a nuclear laser on a tower. Peppino has no choice but to climb the tower. It's very goofy, with its rough graphics and brilliantly funny character designs, but also carefully thought through—there are no lives or health, but there are some really tricky challenges if you want to take them on.

AVAILABLE ON: PC

02 Dave the Diver

■ We've all been waiting for a game that combines fishing, exploration, and restaurant management, and here it is! Dave is a diver who takes on the task of managing a sushi place and catching the fish for it. The fishing mechanic in *Dave the Diver* is quite different from most games—they're basically boss battles you have to prepare for by upgrading your equipment. You can dive in the morning and afternoon, then manage the restaurant at night, unlocking new recipes and drawing in customers. These elements combine to make a brilliantly original game.

AVAILABLE ON:
Nintendo Switch, PC, Mac

01 Sea of Stars

■ The SNES-style pixelated look may remind you of *Stardew Valley*, but this is a huge RPG with a terrific story, great music, and many, many delightful details. It follows two Solstice Warriors—Valere, who uses the power of the moon, and Zale, whose power comes from the sun—as they battle the Fleshmancer, an alchemist who has created the monstrous Dwellers. You can control up to six characters and the turn-based combat—which in some games feels like it's holding up the fun rather than adding to it—is smooth and enjoyable. Its maps are superbly designed and you can't resist exploring them. Five stars out of five!

AVAILABLE ON: Nintendo Switch, PS5, PS4, Xbox Series S/X, Xbox One, PC

SEA OF STARS

THERE'S SO MUCH TO SEA IN THIS MAGIC RETRO RPG!

As this is our number-one indie game of the year, we thought we'd take a closer look at it. *Sea of Stars* came out at almost exactly the same time as the remake of *Super Mario RPG*, and it's very influenced by Japanese console RPGs of the 1990s. It's been a huge hit, which confirms there's still an audience for this style of gaming.

For quite a while, *Sea of Stars* seems to have a pretty standard RPG story—two heroes are the only ones with the magic powers to defeat a looming evil—but stick with it! More characters come into the story, hidden depths are revealed—and without spoiling anything for you, it goes in some pretty interesting directions...

QUICK TIPS

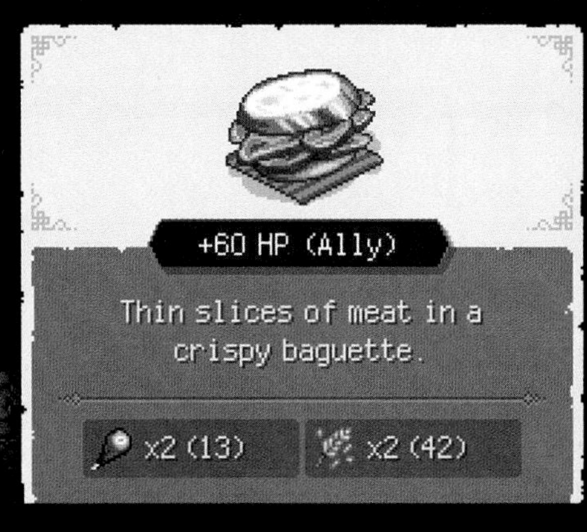

EAT IT

■ Food isn't hard to come by in *Sea of Stars*, so there's no need to hoard it—you have limited inventory space for meals anyway.

REEL TALK

■ When fishing, only use the reel button when your fish enters the safe zone of water in the center. If the fish jumps up, you can stun it with a quick press of the reel.

BE NOSY

■ Always investigate anything that looks like it might be a hidden area. It's just that kind of game! In particular, look out for cracks in the floors.

TURNING UP FOR THE FIGHT

Though it has retro stylings, *Sea of Stars* has some really neat innovations—not least in its turn-based combat, which has more to it than just choosing your next attack…

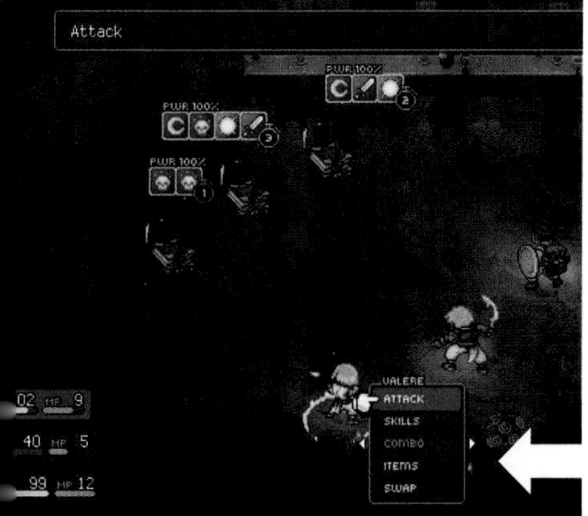

COUNTERATTACKING

And you'll sometimes see a number of icons next to the clock that counts down to a foe unleashing their attack. These are the attacks you have to make to stop them—this is called lock breaking.

TIME IT RIGHT

A correctly timed button press will make hits more effective. And not just hits—blocks, magic, and even food can all be enhanced with perfect timing.

STRONGER TOGETHER

Lock breaking is the most effective way to build combo energy. The game is great at making your party fight as a party, rather than just alongside one another—regular attacks generate live mana, which other characters can use.

RELIC REINFORCEMENTS

Instead of difficulty settings, *Sea of Stars* gives you some Relics for free at the start, which you can choose to turn off or on—so if you're struggling with a tricky boss fight, you always have the option of using Relics.

FAST FACT

***Sea of Stars* is a prequel to *The Messenger*, a retro platform game made by the same developer, Sabotage Studio, which came out in 2018—but you don't need to have played it to get what's going on in *Sea of Stars*!**

LIKE THIS? TRY THIS:

CHRONO TRIGGER

One of the best RPGs of all time and a big influence on *Sea of Stars*, *Chrono Trigger* came out on the SNES in 1995 and has since been released on the Nintendo DS and PlayStation Network—and you can still buy it on Steam, iOS, and Android.

BOOSTING YOUR PARTY IN SEA OF STARS

How to make your band of heroes that bit more legendary!

The thing that really sets an RPG apart from other story-based games is the ability to level up your characters and give them new skills and items. It's an important part of making it feel like they've been on a journey. Here are some things you should know before embarking on *Sea of Stars'* epic quest.

1 Stat up

When leveling up you can pick a bonus stat to increase. We recommend focusing on Physical Defense for Garl, Physical Attack and Defense for Seraï, Speed and Physical Attack for Valere, and Magic Attack for Zale. Boosting HP is a good idea for any character.

2 Don't make it a grind

The amount of EXP you can earn increases with each new area you reach, so there's no need to grind EXP in one area—keep progressing instead. This isn't really a grindy game; it's better to go with the story.

3

Make it count

■ The Abacus may sound like a boring accessory, but it's actually very useful—and much cheaper and easier to obtain than most accessories. It enables you to see the HP of enemies (except bosses), which is very helpful in planning combat strategy! Buy and equip one for your party until you find something more powerful.

ITEM NAME	OWNED	PRICE
Teal Amber Staff	0	48 G
Silver Sword	0	52 G
Basic Armor	2	28 G
Miner's Smock	0	32 G
Abacus	1	36 G
Papillotte	0	
Potato	25	

FAST FACT

Ten tracks on the *Sea of Stars* soundtrack were composed by Yasunori Mitsuda, who also did the music for *Chrono Trigger*. His music also appears in the *Xenoblade Chronicles* series and the anime *Black Butler*.

4

Solutions at sundown

■ Another way to enhance your party is to do the Day & Night puzzles you were shown during the tutorial. Completing one of these gets you a combo move (or sometimes something better). This gives you better options during combat, so never pass up the chance to complete a puzzle!

Here comes the sun

■ Get the most out of Zale's Sunball skill by launching it after it expands for the third time. This is when it's at its largest and most powerful, and will score you a critical hit. But time it right—it shrinks again very quickly and you'll be forced to release it anyway!

5

Underground business

■ A very good place to buy Relics can be found in the port town of Brisk. Swim under the jetty that sticks out straight down at the harbor and you can enter a hidden market. Save your gold for here! To use this shop you'll need the Trader's Signet, which can be found in the Stonemasons Outpost wind caves.

ONE PIECE ODYSSEY

AN RPG MADE FROM MANY PIECES OF *ONE PIECE*!

The saga of Monkey D. Luffy and the Straw Hat Pirates never ends! The *One Piece* manga began in 1997, the anime in 1999, and both are still going—there are over one hundred books and one thousand TV episodes. So, if you want to get into it now, you've got a lot to catch up on!

Thankfully, *One Piece Odyssey* works just fine if you're new to this mega-franchise. It weaves elements from previous stories into a new one by the creator of the series, Eiichiro Oda, to create an ambitious turn-based RPG in the style of the *Dragon Quest* series. The result might just be the best *One Piece* game—and there have been a lot of them!

QUICK TIPS

DON'T KEEP SWITCHING

■ Stick with Luffy unless you need a particular crew member's skills—he's the best for navigating and picking up objects.

DELEGATE TO THE AI

■ Use the Auto Battle and Speed Up options. The choices the AI makes don't make much difference to how the battle goes and will save you a lot of time.

CLICK FOR REWARDS

■ Don't forget to clear each objective as you complete it—like in *Genshin Impact*, you have to confirm each one to get the reward, otherwise they just stack up on your tab!

ALL WASHED UP

The story of *Odyssey* sees Luffy and the Straw Hats marooned and powerless on the island of Waford. You may think shipwrecking our heroes seems an odd choice for a game about pirates—it's called *One Piece*, not *One Place*…

THANKS FOR THE MEMORIES

However, the crew learn they can regain their powers by going to a dimension called Memoria. This lets them revisit classic *One Piece* moments—so, in fact, there's plenty of travel involved.

BACK TO BASICS

This is a clever way of pleasing fans while introducing new players to the series's history—and it means the game has a traditional RPG structure, with the characters starting out weak before leveling up.

STOP AND CHAT

The path through the game is mostly linear, and often you get guided back to it if you stray too far. But, there are parts where you have more freedom to explore, and there's real depth to the locations, with lots of NPCs to talk to.

STRETCH GOALS

The manga is known for its goofy, hilarious fight sequences, and the combat system in *Odyssey* captures this with its lively design and Luffy's stretchy moves.

FAST FACT

One Piece **was the best-selling manga of the year for eleven years in a row, running from 2008 to 2018. It also holds the record for most copies published of any comic by a single author.**

LIKE THIS? TRY THIS:

FIRE EMBLEM: THREE HOUSES

This tactical RPG was the first in the *Fire Emblem* series for a long time. It's not particularly challenging for committed RPG heads, but if *One Piece Odyssey* has got you in the mood for more, this has a great narrative and is surprisingly addictive!

The Wide World of One Piece

Take a piece of these!

■ Outside Japan, other manga and anime are better known than *One Piece*, but in Japan it's huge, and there have been more than fifty games based on the series, beginning with *Become the Pirate King!* from 2000. That was only ever released in Japan (on the WonderSwan, a console that only came out in Japan), and the same is true of many other *One Piece* games—but here are five that made it overseas!

Unlimited World Red (2013)

■ Originally released on the 3DS, this final game in the *Unlimited* series sees the crew getting kidnapped on the Island of Promises, except for Luffy, who must track down and rescue them. The Strong Words system of upgrades is especially fun.

Burning Blood (2016)

■ This fighting game sees characters taking each other on in teams. The combat is a little basic, but the story campaign is better, using the Paramount War arc from the manga. Anyone who hasn't been following the story from the beginning may have no idea what's going on, however!

Grand Cruise (2018)

■ The main selling point of this game is to see the *One Piece* characters in VR. It offers two modes—Sea Battle Against the Navy and Repel the Kraken—but the gameplay in both is very limited, and there's no skill to it at all. One to avoid.

World Seeker (2019)

■ This game provides what many *One Piece* fans have been looking for all along: an open world with the freedom to explore. It's not perfect, but there's some great design and the story feels like classic *One Piece*, as the crew get tricked into visiting an island of pirate prisons and Luffy decides to help the locals get rid of the Marines.

FAST FACT

There are One Piece games in many different genres, including a baseball game, *Going Baseball*, which came out on the Game Boy Advance in 2004—but (you guessed it) only in Japan.

Pirate Warriors 4 (2020)

■ *Odyssey* is the natural successor to the *Pirate Warriors* games, which have generally been the best *One Piece* games—and the fourth in the series is also a good place to start if you're new to this world.

PC GAMING SETUP

EVERYTHING YOU NEED TO RUN TOP GAMES ON A PC!

Games consoles are all designed to play games, but that's not the case with PCs. A lot of computers are only designed to create documents, browse the web, and play videos: they'll be able to run 16-bit games in an emulator, but try to play a new triple-A game and they'll fall over. PCs that can cope with new games will cost more money, so what do you actually need?

Games keep getting more sophisticated and so need more powerful hardware to run. After *Fortnite*'s Chapter 5 update, the minimum spec went up, and it was impossible to run the game on some PCs that coped fine with it before. When buying a new PC, find the requirements for the games you want to play—and if possible, get a setup that's better than the minimum, so it doesn't get outdated right after you buy it!

The three most important elements in a gaming PC are the processor, RAM, and graphics card—if you need to prioritize what warrants the money most, spend it on those three areas.

KEYBOARD

■ Back-lit keyboards are popular in the gaming community. The lights help you see the keys if you've lowered the room lights for atmosphere.

DISPLAY

■ The important thing is for your PC to be able to cope with games—but to be able to really appreciate them, a high-definition display is necessary. And if you're playing on a laptop, you may want to consider a separate monitor that can be plugged in!

PROCESSOR

■ This is the thing that makes programs actually run. The most common processors in PCs are made by Intel, and their most basic processor has a dual core. Higher-spec ones have a quad-core, and the better your processor is, the faster your PC will run and the more tasks it can cope with at once. A high-end processor is strongly recommended for gaming!

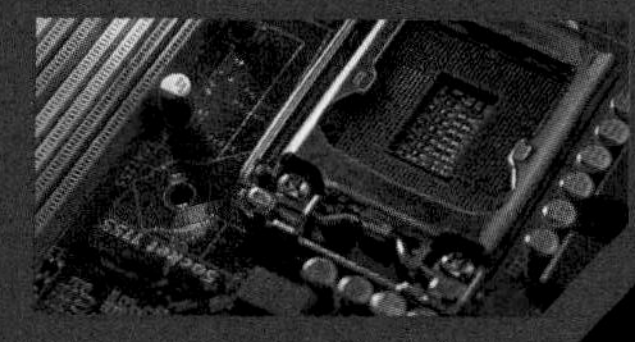

STORAGE

■ Games can take up a lot of space. Again, check how big the games you want to play are, then do some math. If you're only going to be playing a handful of games on your PC, you should be able to cope with a standard hard drive, but if you're looking to store more than a few, go bigger.

GRAPHICS CARD

■ The graphics card is the big difference between a PC used for gaming and one that isn't. The speed and detail of images in modern games needs a higher level of graphics processing. Normal PCs have what's called an integrated graphics card, but a dedicated one is generally considered better for gaming. And check if a PC has its own separate RAM just for video—this is called VRAM, and will also boost gaming performance.

HEADSET

■ When you're playing with friends online, this is an essential part of your gaming kit. The big question is wired or wireless, and a large part of the answer depends on your budget—there are some great wired options that aren't going to break the bank, plus you can generally use these across all platforms, but it's not as straightforward with wireless headsets, so make sure your headset works for all your needs.

RAM

■ It's important to know the difference between the hard drive, which is the memory your computer uses for storage, and the RAM (random access memory), which is used for programs that are running. You might have twenty games stored on your hard drive, but you only play one of them at once—and while it's being played, data that's currently in use is copied to the RAM, where your computer can find it more quickly. Not enough RAM means your game slows down, so the more RAM your PC has, the better.

Unicorn Overlord

Wage war and win back the kingdom!

■ Tactical RPGs combine elements from traditional *Dungeons & Dragons* type RPGs and tabletop strategy games like *Warhammer*. They're not the easiest games to get into, but they became especially popular in Japan in the 1990s with the *Fire Emblem* series.

Games like *Fire Emblem*, *Nobunaga's Ambition*, and *Final Fantasy Tactics* are the inspiration for *Unicorn Overlord*, which aims to capture the gameplay of classic tactical RPGs while being very much its own thing. The developers, Vanillaware, have a good record with this kind of world—they previously made *Dragon's Crown*—and they've spent ten years working on *Unicorn Overlord*!

Striking back at the Empire

■ The continent of Fevrith is split into five nations—Cornia, Drakenhold, Elheim, Bastorias, and Albion. General Valmore has seized the throne of Cornia from Queen Ilenia, exiled Prince Alain, and established the Zenoiran Empire.

Comrades in arms

When Alain is old enough, he determines to build a liberation army to free the continent. His allies include his childhood friend Lex, as well as Josef, the holy knight who trained them both, and Scarlett, priestess of the Palevian Church.

Strength in numbers

New allies can be collected through completing quests. There are more than sixty characters you can add to your army, including elves, beasts, and angels! It's an open world, and you can conquer it back in whatever order you like. Liberating towns will gain access to their resources.

Absolute units

The units you send into battle can be balanced by combining fighters of different classes and skills, and you can give them tactics. Combat also zooms in on individual battles. It all unfolds in real time—but don't panic, because you can pause things to check your position and adjust your strategy.

FAST FACT

To keep things accessible, *Unicorn Overlord* has a Sweet difficulty level for those who are more interested in the story than grinding out victories. There's also Normal mode, and Hard for strategy fans who want a real challenge!

A world in miniature

We really like how the graphics have a tabletop feel. The way some elements are in sharp focus while others aren't makes it look like you're focusing on models rather than looking out over a vast landscape.

FINAL FANTASY VII REBIRTH

NOW THAT'S WHAT WE CALL A GRAND FINALE!

There's no contest: This is the most ambitious remake in the history of gaming. The new version of the 1997 PlayStation game *Final Fantasy VII* expands and reworks the game so completely that it's been split into three separate games. The project was first rumored when a remake of the opening sequence was made for the PS3 in 2005. It was finally announced in 2015, and the first part—*Final Fantasy VII Remake*—came out in 2020. *Rebirth* is the second. So, yeah, this isn't your usual "upgrade the textures and add a new multiplayer mode" remaster. This is BIG.

QUICK TIPS

MINIGAME MADNESS

■ One of the most-loved elements of *Final Fantasy* are the minigames that serve as a goofy change of pace from the main mission. *Rebirth* features a huge number of these: some are updated from the original, some are all-new.

CHOCOBO RACING

■ This was a popular element of the original game, but has been revamped with a much more *Mario Kart* vibe, with a drift control and three laps of the track needed to complete the race!

3D BATTLER

■ This game can be found at the arcade—it used to be turn-based with a rock-paper-scissors-type system for landing blows, but it's now much more action-packed!

WHERE IT'S AT

If you didn't finish, or even play, *Final Fantasy VII Remake*, don't worry—*Rebirth* is designed to work as a standalone game. There's no shared progression between the games, so you can't carry over all your abilities and gear—but there are some extras available to players with save games from *Remake* and its DLC.

LIFE WITH STRIFE

Final Fantasy VII is the story of Cloud Strife, a former soldier who's become a mercenary and joined a group of freedom fighters seeking to overthrow the Shinra Electric Power Company, which controls the city of Midgar.

STEPPING INTO A WIDER WORLD

Remake ended with the characters escaping Midgar. Whereas the first game was based around that location, *Rebirth* has a more open-world approach. *Rebirth* takes the story up to the Forgotten Capital—but as with *Remake*, this doesn't just repeat the story of the original!

GET A MOVE ON

Open-world games have a habit of sending you all over the map, so you'll be glad to know there's a fast-travel system in *Rebirth*! And it lives up to the name—it really is smooth and fast.

HIT THE DECK

One of the coolest additions is an in-game card game, with its own rules—and you can build your own deck and challenge NPCs to matches!

FAST FACT

The *G-Bike* minigame, which also appeared in *Remake*, was so popular following its appearance in the original *Final Fantasy VII*, it was made into a standalone mobile game!

LIKE THIS? TRY THIS:

CRISIS CORE: FINAL FANTASY VII REUNION

If you still need more, try this remaster of the prequel to the original game, which was originally made for the PSP. Unlike *Remake* and *Rebirth*, this version doesn't change the story!

FINAL FANTASY VII

The game that has changed many things for the better...

One aspect of *Rebirth* that makes clear this is a different game from *Remake* is the combat system, which has been further tweaked and refined. These games are about much more than revisiting the past—they keep on evolving.

1

Classic combat

As with *Remake*, the game has Classic and Active modes for battle. In Classic mode, the game's AI guides the characters, leaving you in charge of the overall direction of the battle. This is easier, as well as being more in the classic RPG style.

2

A piece of the action

In Active mode, you take direct control of the characters—switching between them as you prefer—and must block and dodge as well as attack. This is trickier but more exciting! You can further tweak the difficulty with the new Dynamic option alongside the Easy and Normal ones.

3

Combination combat

■ Combat also has a new element in the form of Synergy abilities. You often see this kind of feature in turn-based RPGs—two characters team up to unleash a special attack, such as launching each other at the enemy, pooling their magical powers, or performing a joint rush.

FAST FACT

In 2023, *Final Fantasy VII Rebirth* was named Most Wanted Game at the Golden Joystick Awards, and Most Anticipated Game at the Game Awards.

4

Combat cat

■ Feline fighter Red XIII joined the party as a guest at the end of *Remake*, but in this game he's a fully playable character. He has a Vengeance gauge, which is filled by successfully guarding attacks: you can then get a speed and strength boost by going into Vengeance mode.

Discworld

■ The original *Final Fantasy VII* was a very big game by PS1 standards—it came on three discs. Despite splitting the original game into three for the remake, and being able to use Blu-ray discs with much more storage, the scale and level of detail in *Rebirth* meant it couldn't fit on one disc, and had to be split across two.

5

Joining the team

■ Yuffie, the protagonist of a bonus episode included in the PS5 upgrade of *Remake*, is a full party member here. Her Doppelganger move creates a clone who fights alongside her. She has a Synergy move with Cait Sith, who's also playable in this game: this involves them both using ninja skills.

Star Ocean:

The Second Story R

One story with many, many endings!

The *Star Ocean* series began in the 1990s and was one of the first RPGs to use a social relationship system, where the choices the player makes affect their relationships with other characters—which in turn affects how the game plays out. The sequel, *The Second Story*, expanded on this, and its storyline had a staggering eighty-six different endings!

The Second Story came out in 1999, and plenty of games since then have taken those mind-blowing innovations and run with them. But this new remaster is still an outstanding game, and a must-play for RPG fans!

Worlds collide

The story follows two main characters—Claude, who's from a future human civilization that's expanded out into space, and Rena, who lives on the planet Expel, which has a much less advanced level of technology. This means the game is part science fiction and part fantasy.

Two sides to every story

■ You choose to make Claude or Rena your lead character at the start of the game, but there are twelve playable characters in total and you can't unlock them all unless you play at least twice—once as Claude, once as Rena. You can use the New Game+ option to carry over your levels and equipment on a repeat play.

A world of contrasts

■ As you can see, the remaster takes an interesting approach to the graphics—the environments have been made much more detailed, but the figures are very similar to the pixelated originals, keeping some of that retro vibe. All the voice acting has been rerecorded, too.

Keep it private

■ The character relationships system is accessed by Private Actions. You can start a Private Action in any town: your party will go off to do different things and you, as the main character, can choose to interact with them in different ways.

FAST FACT

The first *Star Ocean* game has also been remastered under the title *First Departure*—this was originally made for the PSP, but was ported over to Switch and PS4 with the option to use the redrawn character portraits from the PSP or original-style art.

Forming bonds

■ As well as changing the story path, bonds can have effects in battles—if your closest friend in the party falls, this will boost your attacks. You can choose not to do Private Actions if you just want to get on with the story, but they hugely increase the replay value of the game!

TOP 10 ANIME GAMES

Ninjas, pirates, and mechas—it's all here!

■ Gamers just can't get enough of anime-based games—which isn't surprising when you consider how big Japan is in the gaming world. But not all of these games do justice to the original stories—so here's a rundown of the very best!

09 Sword Art Online: Fatal Bullet

■ The majority of anime series are based on manga, so *Sword Art Online* is unusual for being based on a series of novels (which have also been turned into manga). But it's perfectly suited to gaming because it's about two gamers playing MMORPGs in virtual reality. *Fatal Bullet* is set in *Gun Gale Online*, a game created for the anime, and actually getting to play one of the games seen in the series will be irresistible to fans.

AVAILABLE ON: **Nintendo Switch, PS4, Xbox One, PC**

10 My Hero One's Justice 2

■ *My Hero Academia*, set in a world of superpowered humans, is one of the most successful manga and anime of recent years, and the *One's Justice* fighting games pit the characters against one another. The second game is fairly similar to the first, but if you're new to these games, this is the one to get—and it really rewards fans of the series.

AVAILABLE ON: **Nintendo Switch, PS4, Xbox One, PC, Stadia**

08 Yu-Gi-Oh! Master Duel

■ *Yu-Gi-Oh!* is most famous as a card game, but there have been several video game versions of it—and *Master Duel* is the best. You can play online against others, acquire new cards, or just play the single-player Story Mode if you prefer. And it's free to play! If you want to play *Yu-Gi-Oh!* digitally, look no further.

AVAILABLE ON: Nintendo Switch, PS5, PS4, Xbox One, Xbox Series S/X, PC, Android, iOS

07 Captain Tsubasa: Rise of New Champions

■ The soccer-themed manga and anime *Captain Tsubasa* was a big hit in the 1980s, and helped make soccer into a much more popular sport in Japan. There have been twenty games based on it, and *Rise of New Champions* is great even if you're not a sports fan, combining enjoyably overdramatic anime elements and the kind of arcade-style action that soccer games used to have before the *FIFA* series went for ultrarealism.

AVAILABLE ON: Nintendo Switch, PS4, PC

06 Gundam Versus

■ *Gundam* is one of the biggest franchises to come from Japan and pretty much created the mecha genre (people piloting giant combat robots, for those who don't know). As well as anime, books, and a lot of plastic kit models, there have been over *two hundred and fifty*—yes, you did read that right!—video games, including puzzle games, soccer games, and kart racers. And this fighting game may be the best of them all!

AVAILABLE ON: PS4

05 One Piece Pirate Warriors 4

■ The all-conquering *One Piece* series of comic fantasy pirate adventures has spawned plenty of video games—we've covered *One Piece Odyssey* elsewhere, but the most popular are the *Pirate Warriors* games, which bring the *One Piece* characters and world into the *Destiny Warriors* series. Choose your character and take on waves of enemies in combat. The story mode also makes a heroic attempt to cram in the plot of the first nine hundred or so episodes of the anime.

AVAILABLE ON: Nintendo Switch, PS4, Xbox One, PC

04 Astro Boy: Omega Factor

■ We've mostly gone for games you can pick up easily today for this list, but we couldn't leave out this one, even though it was only ever released on the Game Boy Advance. Astro Boy has been a huge character since he was created in the 1950s, and *Omega Factor* looks like a straightforward beat-'em-up but has real depth, with references to many other works by his creator, Osamu Tezuka. Get it if you can find it!

AVAILABLE ON:
Game Boy Advance

03 Naruto Shippuden: Ultimate Ninja Storm 4

■ Naruto is the king of martial arts anime, so its stories of ninja training, missions, and competition are obviously suited to video games—there were bound to be some good ones. The *Ultimate Ninja Storm* games are the best, and the fourth in the series sees Naruto and Sasuke fighting in a world war between Shinobi. It's a great multiplayer game and, with over a hundred characters from the series, there's lots to dig into. A remaster of the first three games is also available.

AVAILABLE ON: PS4, Xbox One, PC

02 Jojo's Bizarre Adventure: All Star Battle R

■ The time-spanning craziness of *JoJo's Bizarre Adventure* has made it hugely popular as manga and anime, and its intense rivalries make it perfect for a fighting game. *All-Star Battle R* is a remastered version of a game originally released for the PS3, adding more characters and updating others so they look more like the anime versions. The best thing is how the fighting styles of different characters feature elements from their eras, which really makes it feel like a proper *JoJo* game.

AVAILABLE ON:
Nintendo Switch, PS5, PS4, Xbox Series S/X, Xbox One, PC

01 Dragon Ball FighterZ

■ The *Dragon Ball* series is one of the most popular anime worldwide, especially *Dragon Ball Z*, and *FighterZ* is not just the best anime game, it's one of the best fighting games ever made. Picking a team of three fighters really adds to the variety, because you can combine characters in different ways and develop strategies. The story mode is great and it just captures the vibe of the series perfectly. It's also treated fans well by continuing to release content and giving existing owners a free upgrade to the PS5 and Xbox Series X/S.

AVAILABLE ON:
Nintendo Switch, PS5, PS4, Xbox Series S/X, Xbox One, PC

FAST FACT

***Dragon Ball FighterZ* features an original character, Android 21, whose design was worked on by the creator of the original manga, Akira Toriyama. Toriyama has confirmed the game is an official part of *Dragon Ball* canon.**

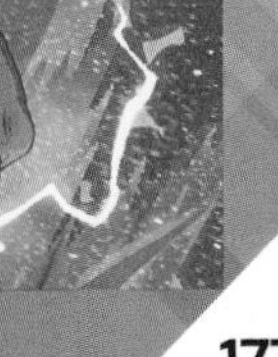

MINECRAFT'S TRAILS AND TALES UPDATE

Ancient things are brought back to life!

The Trails and Tales update is about "self-expression through representation, storytelling, and world-building," according to Mojang. But that's what *Minecraft* has always been about—doing things your way. What elements does this update give players to express themselves with?

CHERRY GROVES

Like meadows, the cherry grove biome spawns in mountain regions, usually lower down but also on plateaus higher up. It contains cherry trees—which in turn means a whole new type of wood. Cherry logs are very dark red on the outside, but create light pink planks.

NEW BLOCKS

Bamboo has also been added, which can be crafted into yellow planks. This is part of the update's focus on decorative items, as bamboo and cherry planks add fresh color to your wood constructions. The smart chiseled bookshelf is another exciting addition—unlike the old bookshelf, it actually holds books!

NEW ANIMAL MOBS

Camels can be ridden, and some hostile mobs can't reach you when you're up on one. Sniffers won the mob vote at Minecraft Live 2022, which led to them being included. These are ancient mobs, thought to be extinct, but if you find and hatch an egg you can bring them back. They're good at sniffing out seeds for decorative plants.

ARCHAEOLOGY

The archaeology system is our favorite part. It fits well with the ancient cities introduced in 2022—there's a structure you can discover called trail ruins. These are villages from a lost civilization, and they generate in biomes with thick forest—jungle, the old growth biomes, and taiga biomes.

SEEMS SUSPICIOUS

Suspicious gravel generates in trail ruins, as well as in ocean ruins. There's also suspicious sand which can be found under desert pyramids. Both types of suspicious block drop nothing if broken—but a feather, copper ingot, and stick can be crafted into a brush.

A BRUSH WITH HISTORY

Using this brush on a suspicious block will drop loot. This might be a candle, stained glass, emerald, gold, a smithing template for armor, or a pottery sherd. There are twenty types of sherd to find, and four sherds can be crafted back into a decorative pot!

FAST FACT

Why is it a "sherd" and not a "shard"? Well, we use "shard" to mean a sharp fragment of glass, metal, or china, but in archaeology they use "sherd" to mean broken pieces of pottery.

TEKKEN 8

BACK FOR YET ANOTHER ROUND!

There's been a huge gap between *Tekken* games—*Tekken 7* came out in 2015—but the series celebrated its thirtieth birthday in 2024, so there really had to be a new game to mark the occasion.

The *Tekken* series is heavily associated with the PlayStation—until *Tekken 6*, you couldn't play them on any other home console—and *Tekken 8* is their first game for the PS5, using the Unreal Engine 5. It's the first major fighting game to use it, and as well as bringing more cinematic animations, it has a whole new level of detail, with rain and sweat rolling down the characters' faces!

QUICK TIPS

STATUS UPDATE

■ Training mode includes the ability to save a particular status in a fight and return to it—excellent for practicing specific moves and techniques.

SMASH OR DASH

■ Always try to execute a Heat Smash or Heat Dash when your Heat bar is almost empty—these moves will take you out of Heat mode, so this is the best time!

DON'T SWEAT THE TECHNIQUES

■ As well as a complete move list for each character, the game includes a Main Techniques tab that lists the most useful ones and what they do—very handy information!

THE HEAT IS ON

Tekken 8's gameplay changes reward players who go on the attack rather than sitting back and waiting for opponents to make a move. The major new element is the Heat system.

HIT THE BAR

You can activate a Heat Burst at any time in a match, and then go into Heat mode after your next attack (whether it connects or not). Heat moves are powered by the Heat bar—and you only get one of these per round!

CHIPPING AWAY

Heat mode enhances your attack, and means you do chip damage when your opponent blocks—so the opponent still takes a little damage (though this only becomes permanent with a follow-up attack).

SMASHING IT

The Rage mechanic from *Tekken 7*, which enabled players low on health to make a comeback, is still present but has been modified: the Rage Drive has been made into part of the Heat system, Heat Smash.

OVER IN A DASH

Executing a Heat Smash ends Heat mode, no matter how full your Heat bar is. The same is true of Heat Dash, which you can do by holding forward. These are powerful abilities, but use them wisely!

FAST FACT

***Tekken* is one of many iconic PlayStation games referenced in the PS5 launch game *Astro's Playroom*. It's near the start of Mt. Motherboard—look to the left when you get there.**

LIKE THIS? TRY THIS:

POKKÉN TOURNAMENT DX

It's got a very different look to *Tekken*, but this *Pokémon* fighting game copies the gameplay quite closely—that's why it's called *Pokkén*! It's a great choice for Switch owners who are frustrated that *Tekken* and *Street Fighter* aren't available on the console.

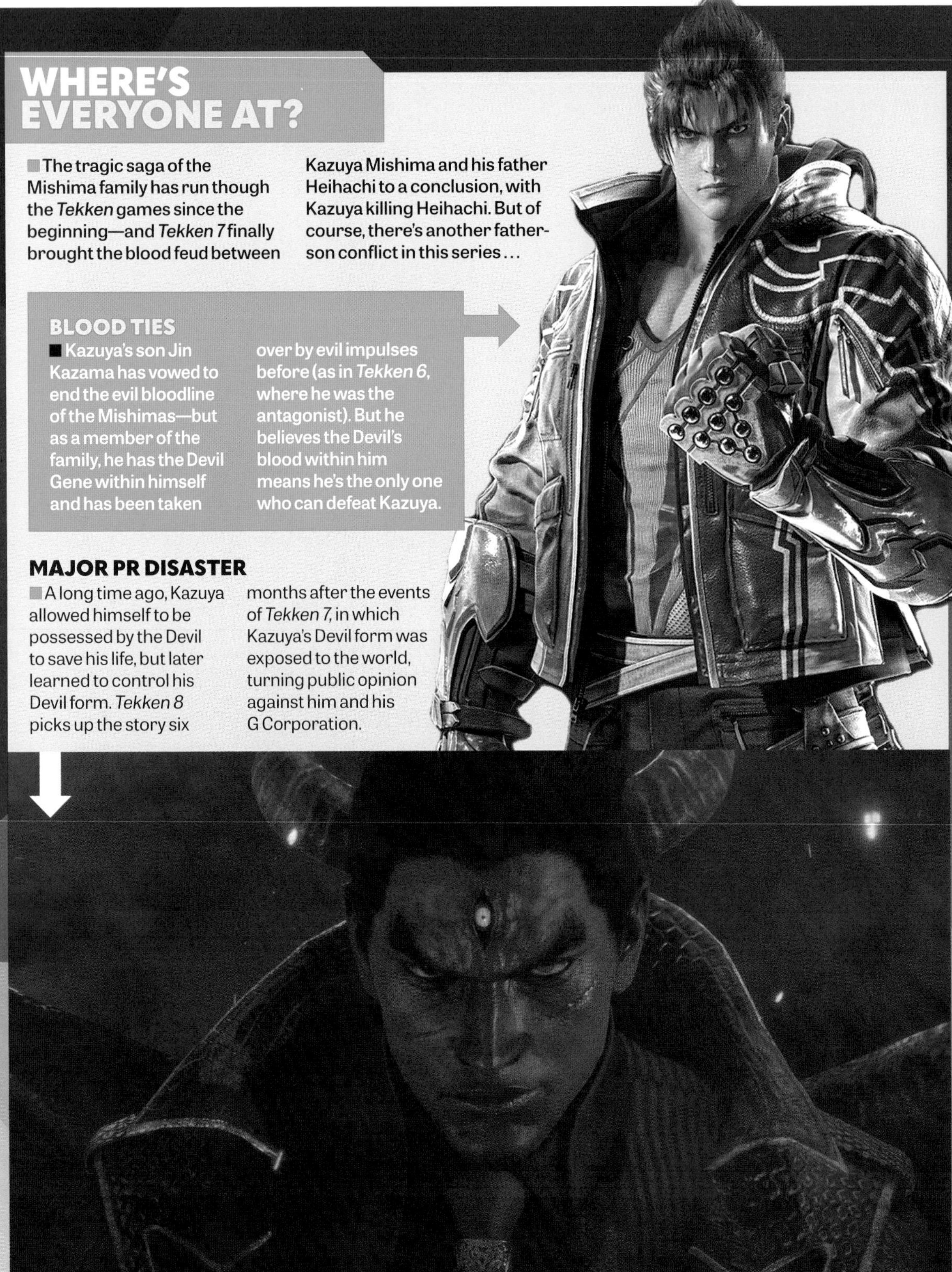

WHERE'S EVERYONE AT?

The tragic saga of the Mishima family has run though the *Tekken* games since the beginning—and *Tekken 7* finally brought the blood feud between Kazuya Mishima and his father Heihachi to a conclusion, with Kazuya killing Heihachi. But of course, there's another father-son conflict in this series . . .

BLOOD TIES

Kazuya's son Jin Kazama has vowed to end the evil bloodline of the Mishimas—but as a member of the family, he has the Devil Gene within himself and has been taken over by evil impulses before (as in *Tekken 6*, where he was the antagonist). But he believes the Devil's blood within him means he's the only one who can defeat Kazuya.

MAJOR PR DISASTER

A long time ago, Kazuya allowed himself to be possessed by the Devil to save his life, but later learned to control his Devil form. *Tekken 8* picks up the story six months after the events of *Tekken 7*, in which Kazuya's Devil form was exposed to the world, turning public opinion against him and his G Corporation.

CHARACTER COUNT

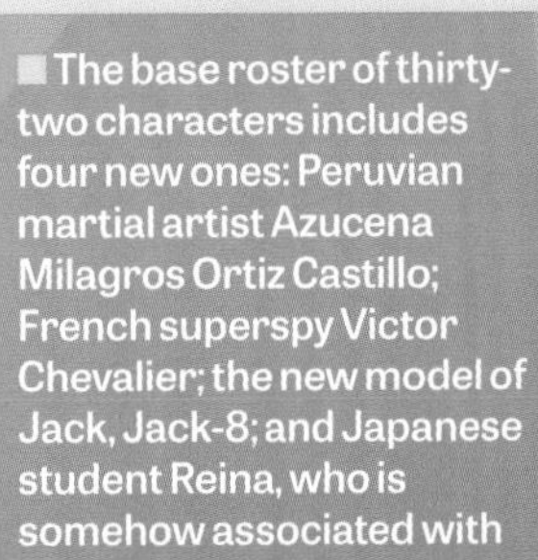

The base roster of thirty-two characters includes four new ones: Peruvian martial artist Azucena Milagros Ortiz Castillo; French superspy Victor Chevalier; the new model of Jack, Jack-8; and Japanese student Reina, who is somehow associated with the Mishimas...

CORPORATE CONFLICT

The war between G Corp and Heihachi's Mishima Zaibatsu has already had a terrible impact on the world. As the United Nations discusses what action to take against G Corp, Kazuya arrives, saying he has no intention of stopping—and then setting G Corp's private army on New York City!

FAST FACT

Sales of the *Tekken* games have kept going up as the series has continued—*Tekken 7* outsold all previous games, shifting over nine million copies!

MOTHER'S HOME

Tekken 8 sees the return of Jun Kazama, Jin's mother! Missing and thought dead since *Tekken 2*, when she was attacked by Ogre, she is back in the story—and as a playable character. Jin has often held on to her memory to stave off his Devil form—and her own bloodline has the power to neutralize it...

Prince of Persia: The Lost Crown

These rides defy the laws of physics!

■ *Prince of Persia* has an important place in gaming history—the original 1989 game was the first platform game to use realistic movement and gravity rather than the cartoonish feel of *Mario*-type platformers, creating a cinematic feel with smooth animation. It's where today's hyperrealistic action games started!

The series had great success in the 1990s and 2000s, plunging players into a world of magic and ancient evil—and the 2003 entry *The Sands of Time* has been described as one of the all-time great games. But, after 2010's *The Forgotten Sands*, the series seemed to be . . . well . . . forgotten. *The Lost Crown* is the first major *Prince of Persia* game since then. Is it back with a bang?

Just in time

■ *The Lost Crown* features a new protagonist, Sargon, who's the youngest member of a group known as the Immortals. Sargon's ability to manipulate time comes in handy when the Immortals arrive at Mount Qaf to rescue a prince, only to discover the place is cursed and time doesn't flow properly here.

FAST FACT

There was another *Prince of Persia* game in the works in the early 2010s, called *Prince of Persia: Redemption*. It was canceled, but test footage has surfaced on YouTube.

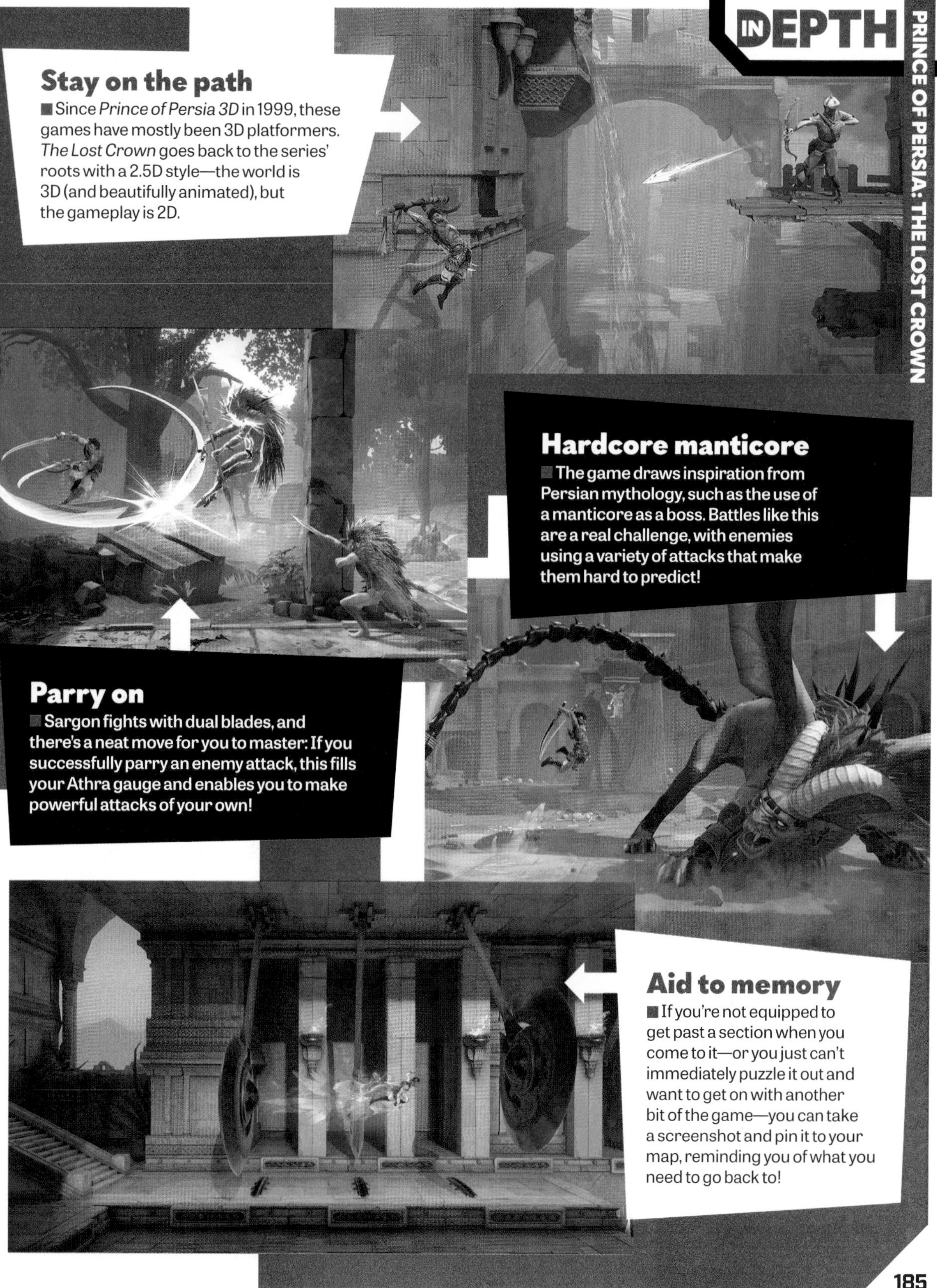

Stay on the path

Since *Prince of Persia 3D* in 1999, these games have mostly been 3D platformers. *The Lost Crown* goes back to the series' roots with a 2.5D style—the world is 3D (and beautifully animated), but the gameplay is 2D.

Hardcore manticore

The game draws inspiration from Persian mythology, such as the use of a manticore as a boss. Battles like this are a real challenge, with enemies using a variety of attacks that make them hard to predict!

Parry on

Sargon fights with dual blades, and there's a neat move for you to master: If you successfully parry an enemy attack, this fills your Athra gauge and enables you to make powerful attacks of your own!

Aid to memory

If you're not equipped to get past a section when you come to it—or you just can't immediately puzzle it out and want to get on with another bit of the game—you can take a screenshot and pin it to your map, reminding you of what you need to go back to!

HAWKED

Forget robots in disguise—this is all-out war!

It's tough to challenge *Fortnite*, but *HAWKED* pulls off the trick of being similar enough to appeal to fans of the dominant PvP shooter while offering something different. It's got a very *Fortnite*-y look, with players able to adopt flashy and goofy styles, and it's all set on an island where you must open chests and load up with weapons after arriving. But it's an extraction game, with the focus on treasure hunting and getting out with the loot. Its mix of game elements makes it frantic and fun!

CLAIM YOUR REWARD

■ The Artifacts translate into skills and buffs you can equip for another run. You can use this to give your team different and complementary abilities—which is another way it differs from *Fortnite*, where every player starts the match exactly the same.

PEW

ALTERNATIVE STRATEGY

■ There's also a second Artifact that the lizards have already grabbed, so you can try for that. But, the problem is, other teams will undoubtedly have the same idea, and you'll have to fend them off as well as the lizards!

THE POWER OF THREE

■ Players drop onto the island in teams of three—there are ten teams in each round. The island is also inhabited by lizard monsters, and you're all searching for valuable magical Artifacts—one of which is inside a vault.

FAST FACT

HAWKED supports cross-platform play, but unlike _Fortnite_, you can't access the same account from different platforms, so pick the one you want to play on and stick with it!

RACE FOR THE PRIZE

■ The game can change in an instant—you can be in the middle of solving a puzzle, but when you get a GRAIL alert, you have to drop it because that means another team has solved all theirs and is heading for the extraction point! When it gets to this stage, you need to head out and stop them!

GLYPH IT UP

■ To get your hands on Artifacts, you need Glyphs—and you get Glyphs by solving puzzles. This is the main way of winning a round. Or you can just wipe out all the other players and win that way!

THE BEST SPACE GAMES

THEY'RE OUT OF THIS WORLD!

The very earliest video games were either about tennis or spaceships. Way back in 1962, one of the most important games ever was created—*Spacewar!*, in which two spaceships battled each other in . . . well . . . space. And while tennis doesn't dominate the gaming world in the same way as it did in the era of *Pong*, we're still fascinated by games that take us into space, allowing us to explore its infinite wonders and blow stuff up. Here's a rundown of the best!

10 STAR CONFLICT

This free-to-play MMO has several different modes—you can jump into battles with other players, take on NPC enemies in co-op missions, attempt to conquer regions on behalf of a Corporation, or explore the game's open world. The best part is the sheer number of spaceships. There are four types—interceptors, fighters, frigates, and destroyers—but over one hundred different ships to find and unlock!

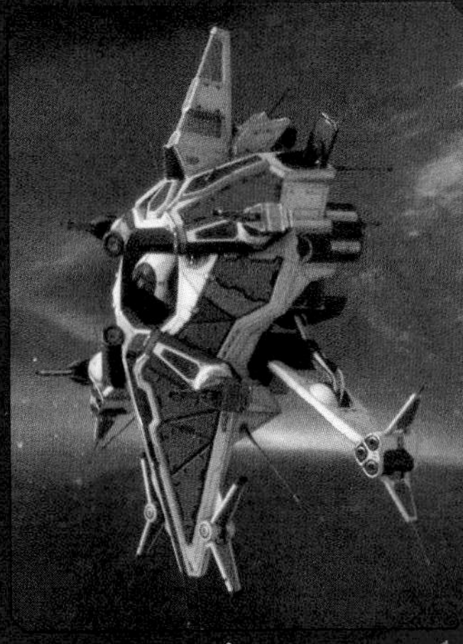

9 STAR FOX

Star Fox—about a spaceship fighter pilot who is also a fox—stunned SNES gamers in the 1990s with its revolutionary 3D polygon graphics. Nothing like this had ever been seen on a console, and its animal characters made it feel like a uniquely Nintendo take on *Star Wars*–style action. The most recent game was *Star Fox Zero* on the Wii U—it's a mystery why this series hasn't made it to the Switch!

8 STAR TREK: BRIDGE CREW

There's always been a big overlap between *Star Trek* fans and PC gamers, and projects like the *Star Trek Online* MMORPG have developed successfully. *Bridge Crew* is a great place to start if you're new to *Star Trek* games—it was designed for VR headsets, but a non-VR version followed. It really captures the feel of being in the *Star Trek* universe, taking your place on the bridge of the USS *Aegis* and playing your part in missions.

7 ELITE DANGEROUS

The original *Elite* game came out way back in 1984, and its simulation of space travel and exploration—plus its open-ended gameplay—meant it was a big influence on the games that came after, including several on this list. While the series vanished after a third game in the 1990s, it was rebooted very successfully with *Elite Dangerous* in 2014, winning back its place among the greatest space games.

6 STELLARIS

This is what's known as a 4X strategy game, which means it's based around four activities: exploring, expanding, exploiting, and exterminating. It has several cool aspects, such as the three different types of interstellar travel you can chose from at the start of a game—warp, wormhole, and hyperspace. Each new game will unfold very differently depending on your choice!

5 FTL: FASTER THAN LIGHT

■ This indie game has been around for a while but still has a keen fan base. It's a strategy game, but also takes inspiration from dungeon crawlers. You're in command of one spaceship seeking to deliver important information to its fleet, tackling enemies and other obstacles along the way, and it has a very *Star Wars* and *Star Trek* feel. It's a challenging game though!

4 OUTER WILDS

■ In this game you can explore an entire star system . . . but you only have twenty-two minutes to do it. At that point the system's star goes supernova. However, there's a time loop that sends you back to the start, so you can explore again with the knowledge you picked up on previous runs. Through exploring and solving logic puzzles you can learn the secrets of the Nomai and work out why the time loop is happening. It's ingenious and highly original! Count it among the greatest space games.

3 KERBAL SPACE PROGRAM

■ This looks wacky, but once you get past its little green alien characters, it's actually the most realistic space game around. No, really. It's a flight simulator where you have to build and launch your own spacecraft (there are several different types), and it uses accurate physics—so just getting your ship off the ground requires you to learn how these things work in real life. *Kerbal Space Program* has been praised by space industry professionals for helping people understand the reality of space travel, making this an educational game that's also great fun!

2 EVE ONLINE

Any MMORPG that's kept players coming back for more than two decades must be doing something right. The universe of *Eve Online* contains more than 7,800 star systems, and as well as exploring, mining, and building, players can interact in complex ways—trading, forming alliances, declaring war, and more. But be careful out there—pirates lurk in the space ways, and in many corners of the universe, crime is a way of life!

1 NO MAN'S SKY

No Man's Sky truly captures the size of space: it takes place in a procedurally generated universe that just keeps on going, meaning it contains 18 quintillion planets. The game was hyped up before release, and got a mixed response—but a series of updates added new features and fixes, and it became the game we wanted it to be! There's a story to follow and complete—the Artemis Path—but the game has so much more to offer, including an online multiplayer mode that's flourished in the years since it first came out and is now the best place for space-based co-op and competition.

FAST FACT

The soundtrack of *No Man's Sky*, created by the post-rock group 65daysofstatic, also works procedurally—the game combines the sounds and melodies recorded by the group in different ways depending on what's happening in the game!

Fantasy Life i: The Girl Who Steals Time

This innovative mash-up is time well spent!

■ The original *Fantasy Life* came out for the Nintendo 3DS way back in 2012, combining *Animal Crossing*-style life sim with *Zelda*-style RPG. You took on one of 12 life classes (jobs) and gradually leveled up to unlock new items and tasks—while also investigating the strange purple meteorites that fell on the world of Reveria.

As the series moves to the Switch for *The Girl Who Steals Time*, it also moves to a new location—the ruined Mysteria Island. The game was due out in 2023, but was put back a year so the development team could work on it some more, so was it worth a twelve-year wait?

New Looks

■ *The Girl Who Steals Time* has made many improvements on the original. The character creation screen has way more options, and you can see these options laid out much more clearly. It has a very Nintendo Mii-like feel.

Making Plans

The island setting makes it feel like *Animal Crossing: New Horizons*, and the options to customize the environment are more extensive. You can place furniture outside and design the whole town yourself. The landscape can be reworked, too, employing this guy who reminds us of the robot from *Laputa: Castle in the Sky*.

New Strength

Your Strength Points, which are essential to all kinds of actions, used to go down when you dashed (like the stamina wheel in *Zelda*), making exploration slower. But now they're not affected by dashing and you can reserve them for combat!

Farm or Paint

The original twelve life classes are all still there—Alchemist, Tailor, Cook, Blacksmith, Carpenter, Paladin, Mercenary, Magician, Hunter, Angler, Miner, and Woodcutter—but now they've been joined by two new classes: Artist and Farmer. You're free to switch between jobs, so you're not stuck with one once you've chosen it.

Level-5, the studio that makes the *Fantasy Life* games, is best known for the *Professor Layton* series of puzzle games, including a crossover with the *Ace Attorney* series. A new game, *Professor Layton and the New World of Steam*, is in the works!

I'm going to send you back a thousand years.

Back in Time

But what about the story side? Well, it involves moving between two time periods—the present, and a thousand years ago. Mysterious Strangelings appear on the island in the past, which may be possessed by the spirits of the dead . . . Can you save them?

TOP 10 CO-OP GAMES

Now, you kids play nice together, OK?

■ There are so many different types of co-op gaming—you may be fighting alongside each other, trying to create something together or looking to solve a puzzle. If you're looking for a new game to be sociable with, check out this list . . .

10 Goat Simulator 3

■ *Goat Simulator 3* is the sequel to *Goat Simulator*. There is no *Goat Simulator 2*, which gives you some idea of how silly this game is. You play as a goat and create havoc in an urban area, and it's not hard to see how that becomes even more fun in co-op mode. There are some neat multiplayer minigames, too.

AVAILABLE ON:
PS5, Xbox Series S/X, PC

09 Sonic Mania

■ This retro entry in the *Sonic* series uses the same two-player gameplay as *Sonic 2*, so as well as competing against each other, a second player can take control of Tails and join the adventure. This is very, very useful in boss fights! You can also unlock & Knuckles mode, which adds Knuckles as a second character.

AVAILABLE ON:
Nintendo Switch, PS4, Xbox One, PC

08 Donkey Kong: Tropical Freeze

■ Many of the *Mario* games feature co-op gameplay, but this platform adventure is one of the best. It sees Donkey Kong seeking to regain control of Donkey Kong Island. In single-player mode you get a companion who can help you, but there's always the option for a second player to take control of them. They can choose between Diddy Kong, Dixie Kong, and Cranky Kong.

AVAILABLE ON: Nintendo Switch, Wii U

07 Castle Crashers

■ An underrated game that came out awhile back, *Castle Crashers* is still around in remastered form—and it's awesome fun in co-op mode. It's a sideways-scrolling hack-and-slash game where you play as knights setting out to rescue four princesses and find a mystical gem. In co-op mode, you progress at the level of the player who's furthest ahead, so everyone can go through it together!

AVAILABLE ON: Nintendo Switch, PS4, Xbox One, PC, Mac

06 Cuphead

■ *Cuphead* is a modern classic, but its boss fights are notoriously tough. So they should be easier in two-player co-op, right? Wrong! The bosses have increased health, so playing together is an even bigger challenge, especially if one of you has less experience with the game. But if a friend does take up that second controller to play as Mugman, you can be sure of getting a real sense of achievement if you make it to those closing credits together.

AVAILABLE ON: Nintendo Switch, PS4, Xbox One, PC, Mac

05 Overcooked!

■ A game that's stressful and frustrating and yet you can't stop playing it. You can tackle *Overcooked!* and its DLC or sequel on your own, swapping between control of two chefs, but it was inspired by teams of chefs working in busy kitchens, juggling different tasks and trying not to let anything drop, so it was always going to work best in multiplayer mode. Perfect if you feel like you don't shout at your friends and family often enough!

AVAILABLE ON: Nintendo Switch, PS5, PS4, Xbox Series X/S, Xbox One, PC, Stadia

04 Risk of Rain 2

■ When you're stranded on an alien planet and you need to kill monsters and find loot, you could really use some help from your friends—so it's a good thing *Risk of Rain 2* gives you exactly that option. It's simple and, yes, repetitive—you fight, you find loot, you upgrade, you repeat— but it's perfectly done and in co-op it becomes nicely messy and chaotic, with the carnage turned right up.

AVAILABLE ON: Nintendo Switch, PS4, Xbox One, PC, Stadia

03 Stardew Valley

■ The all-conquering king of farm sims was launched as a single-player game, but a multiplayer mode was always planned and when this launched, it gave the game a new dimension. You can build cabins on your farm and invite up to three friends to join you there, online or in local split screen. It's perfectly suited to this kind of play, as you can divide up tasks depending on what you prefer doing, or take turns. Just don't log off with anything important still in your inventory! Everyone else hates when you do that.

AVAILABLE ON: Nintendo Switch, PS4, Xbox One, PC, Mac, Android, iOS

02 Portal 2

■ The *Portal* games are absolute classics of the puzzle-platform genre: you change the game area by placing portals that let you move through it in different ways. Like a lot of sequels to single-player games, *Portal 2* added a multiplayer mode. While many co-op games just have you working together on the same campaign as the single-player version, the co-op campaign in *Portal 2* is a whole different story, a sequel to the main one. Both games were reissued as *Portal Companion Collection* for the Switch.

AVAILABLE ON:
Nintendo Switch, PS3, Xbox 360, PC, Mac

FAST FACT

Another mini-entry into the *Portal* franchise came in 2015, when *LEGO Dimensions* included a *Portal 2* level in its main game. The expansion pack, with its Chell minifigure, unlocked a whole extra LEGO *Portal* adventure!

01 It Takes Two

■ As its title suggests, it's a two-player game without a single-player option. You can play together online or locally, but you *have* to work together. The main characters are divorcing parents who end up in the bodies of dolls their daughter has made, and who must find their way back to their normal selves. Almost everything you do involves teamwork—even when playing online, you can see what the other player is doing. Each stage grants you different skills, so there's a huge amount of variety. Put your friendship to the test!

AVAILABLE ON:
Nintendo Switch, PS5, PS4, Xbox Series X/S, Xbox One, PC

Apollo Justice: Ace Attorney Trilogy

Three great games in one? No objections here!

Following on from 2019's *Phoenix Wright: Ace Attorney Trilogy*, which remastered the first three games in the much-loved courtroom visual novel series, this package collects the next three: *Apollo Justice: Ace Attorney*, *Phoenix Wright: Ace Attorney—Dual Destinies*, and *Phoenix Wright: Ace Attorney—Spirit of Justice*.

If you've played an *Ace Attorney* game you'll know what to expect—you're a defense attorney examining evidence, questioning witnesses in the courtroom, and looking for inconsistencies that will disprove the cases against your clients. This is a consistently high-quality series, and it's great they're all being kept available for gamers to access on today's consoles.

Young Justice

Young attorney Apollo Justice takes the lead role in the first game in this collection, due to Phoenix having lost his license to practice law. Phoenix finds himself under suspicion and, in a peculiar twist, designs a whole new trial system in which Apollo must serve as defense.

Cykes you out

Dual Destinies sees the attorneys battling corruption and abuse of the legal system—one client is the mayor, who's been accused of murder. The game introduces a new character, Athena Cykes, whose special skill is detecting conflicting emotions in witnesses who are hiding something.

No defense

In *Spirit of Justice*, Phoenix finds himself in the kingdom of Khura'in, where the legal system doesn't bother with defense attorneys, instead arriving at a verdict by the Divination Séance, a mystical ceremomy. At least it's business as usual back at the Wright Anything Agency!

Create a scene

New extras for this edition include an art library filled with sketches, background art, and more—plus an animation studio where you can create your own *Ace Attorney* scenes, putting the familiar characters in whatever bizarre situations you can imagine!

FAST FACT

In the English language versions of *Ace Attorney*, the setting was changed from Japan to the United States—though the Japanese legal system had to be kept, along with certain Japanese cultural elements. In later games, these oddities were explained by the games taking place in an alternative universe where California is more Japanese-influenced.

Ace tunes

Another new extra, the Orchestra Hall, allows you to listen to the soundtracks of all three games, plus recordings from two special concerts of *Ace Attorney* music and two new tracks—175 tracks in all, and with dancing chibi versions of the characters.

STEAMWORLD BUILD

THIS SERIES IS GATHERING STEAM!

The popular *SteamWorld* series goes back to 2010, when *SteamWorld Tower Defense* was released on the Nintendo DS. Since then, more games have been set in its steampunk postapocalyptic world inhabited by robots: the *SteamWorld Dig* platform games, turn-based strategy game *SteamWorld Heist*, and deck-building RPG *SteamWorld Quest: Hand of Gilgamech*.

Now they've brought us something really different. At the start, *SteamWorld Build* offers a pretty standard, accessible take on city building, but it develops into something more complex later on! It mixes gameplay from tycoons and dungeon crawlers—and even goes back to the roots of the series with tower defense elements!

QUICK TIPS

TAKE A TUMBLE

The tumbleweeds aren't just there for atmosphere—if you click on them, they'll explode and give you a reward! Check the walls and ledges of the map in case some have gotten stuck there.

SPEEDY SERVICE

The Service Inhabitants item is much more useful than it might seem! Equip it to a service building and it will increase the number of Steambots there.

GRAB GOLD

Apart from money, the best resources to collect are gold, tools, charcoal, boards, and vectron parts. Vectron parts are particularly important as you get into the final stages!

INTO THE BADLANDS

SteamWorld Build is set in an environment that's a lot like the Wild West, except for the "minor" detail that everyone's a steam-driven robot. It's a world of railroads, saloons, prospectors, and sheriffs! And monsters . . .

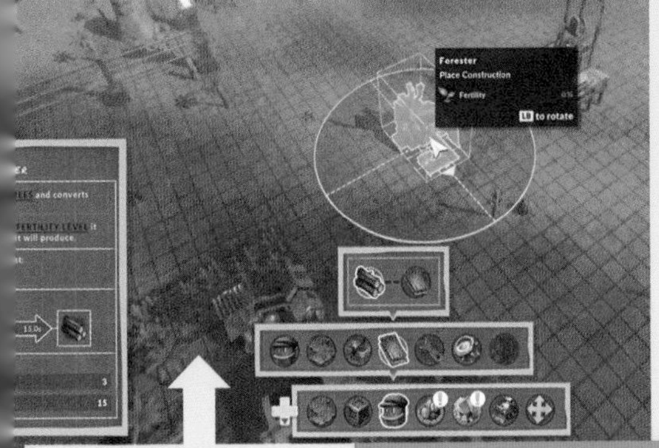

CLEAR THE WAY

Expanding the mine isn't a hassle-free job! There are monsters roaming the depths who don't want you there, and they attack in waves—this is where the dungeon-crawling and tower defense aspects come in!

REAP THE REWARDS

A large amount of *SteamWorld Build* is about setting up systems to gather resources, which you can refine and use to expand your settlement. Once something is set up, it keeps delivering resources. This is what makes it like a tycoon game—you can leave those idle while you work on other areas.

GO UNDERGROUND

Eventually you unlock the underground area of the game and you can start your mine! The mine has its own management requirements and needs resources from the city, but it also generates resources that benefit the city.

REACH FOR THE STARS

A lot of city-building games don't have an endpoint—you just expand your city and keep managing it until you're bored. But the ultimate aim of this game is to build a space rocket!

FAST FACT

SteamWorld Build **takes place at the same time as** ***SteamWorld Dig 2*****, in which the planet becomes unstable and explodes. This is the story of how the escape rocket is built.**

LIKE THIS? TRY THIS:

THE COLONISTS

If you want another city-building game with robots, but prefer something a little calmer, try this cute game. It's about a bunch of robots who just want to be human, setting up home on another planet!

FOUNDING YOUR CITY IN STEAMWORLD BUILD

Get buildin'! Time's a-wastin'!

SteamWorld Build may be a lighter version of a city-building game, but it's got quirks of its own that aren't necessarily obvious to new players. Here are some tips to get you started.

1 Urban planning

Residential and service buildings need to be near one another, so the residents can use the services. Refineries can be placed away from the other two types—but they do need to be near warehouses.

2 Ship out your excess

There's a cap on the amount of resources you can store, and sources of resources will often produce more than you need—that's why unlocking the train station at Milestone 3 is so important. This opens up trade, and you should sell any resources you're overproducing. Make sure your warehouses are connected to the train station with roads, too!

Deliver results

■ Each warehouse initially only has one Steambot making deliveries, and when too many refineries are depending on one warehouse, delivery times will slow down. You can build another warehouse, but it's better to get upgrades for the ones you have first—either from the train station, or from chests while mining. Don't forget to equip these upgrades, as they won't happen automatically!

Milestones aren't millstones

■ The population milestones unlock new buildings—but also new needs for your citizens. You might feel like delaying a milestone is a good idea, until you're ready to tackle this new need—but don't worry! Your citizens' happiness may seem to drop, but population and income won't drop with them, so there's no real downside to passing a milestone.

Roadworthy

■ When you reach Milestone 6 you'll get access to paved roads. You should consider upgrading your dirt roads to paved. This will extend the reach of your service buildings—dirt roads have a range of twenty-four tiles, but paved ones have a range of thirty-eight, so you'll get more value out of services. Later you get maglev roads, which have a range of forty-two. Improving the roads around each warehouse will also make deliveries much faster.

Overexpansion

■ Later in the game, you may find you've built too many residential buildings and you don't have the resources to support them. This isn't a difficult problem to solve—you just need to increase production of the necessary resources—but watch out for it!

FAST FACT

The first 3D entry in the *SteamWorld* series, the co-op action adventure *SteamWorld Headhunter*, picks up where both *Dig 2* and *Build* leave off.

Penny's Big Breakaway

Yo, yo, check this out!

■ When the developers behind *Sonic Mania* didn't get picked to work on *Sonic Superstars*, they set to work on this game instead. There's certainly a *Sonic* feel to *Penny's Big Breakaway*, with its rolling action and tinkling collectible coins—but unlike *Mania*, this is a 3D platformer. The *Sonic* games have had mixed success in 3D, and perhaps that's why the team created their own game engine for *Penny's Big Breakaway*, looking for a new way to make fast platforming action work in a 3D world. Is this the great 3D *Sonic* game we could have had?

String along

■ Penny, an ambitious street performer in the world of Macaroon, responds to Eddie the Emperor's call for new entertainers for his court—but she has a mishap with some Cosmic String and her yo-yo comes to life.

Causing a flap

Yo-Yo has a hunger for snacks and isn't easy to control, and Penny gets on the wrong side of the Emperor when Yo-Yo eats his clothes! Naturally, the Emperor sends his penguin army after Penny, who must flee through twelve different worlds and seek the secret of the Cosmic String.

New tricks

There are many inventive ways Penny can use Yo-Yo—as a weapon, a lasso, a unicycle, a zip line, a helicopter… It's a simple mechanic, but adds so much variety to the game!

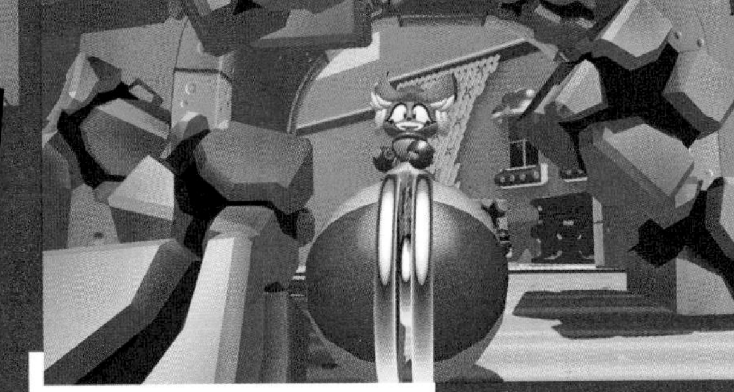

Need for speed

Adding to the *Sonic* feel, the levels are designed so they can be speedrun and there's a time attack mode that comes with online leaderboards. But there's also a main story mode that focuses on progression and leveling up Yo-Yo.

FAST FACT

Christian Whitehead, the lead developer of *Sonic Mania* and *Penny's Big Breakaway*, also worked on the retro platformer *Freedom Planet 2*, which came out on Windows in 2022 and launched on consoles in 2024.

Color wheel

Everything about this game gives us 1990s Sega vibes—the colors are like the original *Sonic the Hedgehog*, and its weird, groovy world is like a cross between the *Disney Illusion* games and *Space Channel 5*. Maybe retro 3D games will be the next big thing!

GLOSSARY

4K
A screen or image with an ultra-high-definition resolution, giving the picture even more detail than a high-definition (HD) image.

Achievement
An award added to your online profile for completing goals or objectives in a game.

AI
Artificial intelligence. Intelligent behavior simulated by a computer to, for instance, control how enemies behave toward a player, or control other players on your team in a sports game.

Battle royale
A type of action game where sixty or more players are dropped onto a single, large map and fight until just one survives.

Beat-'em-up
A fighting game, where two or more fighters battle in hand-to-hand combat.

Boss
A bigger, tougher enemy that players have to fight at the end of a level or mission in a game.

Unicorn Overlord

Campaign
A series of levels or objectives connected by some kind of story, usually making up the single-player mode of a game.

CCG
Collectible card game. A style of game based on real-world card games, where players collect an army of cards and use them to battle other players.

Checkpoint
A point in a game where your progress is saved. If you die, you'll return to the checkpoint.

Combo
In a fighting game or action game, a series of button presses that triggers a hard-hitting attack or counterattack.

Co-op
A game or game mode where players can work together to complete objectives or win the game.

CPU
Central processing unit. The main processor of a computer or games console that does most of the work of running games.

Crafting
Using materials collected within a game to make useful items, armor, or weapons.

Cutscene
An animated sequence or video sequence in a game, used to build atmosphere or tell the story.

Dragon Ball FighterZ

DLC
Downloadable content. Additional items, characters, or levels for a game that you can buy and download as extras.

Easter egg
A secret feature or item that's been hidden in a game, either for fun or as a reward for observant fans.

Endgame
A part of a game that you can carry on playing after you've completed the main campaign or story.

FPS
First-person shooter. A style of game where players move around a map, shooting enemies from a first-person perspective, with a view straight from the hero's eyes.

GPU
Graphics processing unit. The chip inside a computer or console that turns instructions from the game software into 2D or 3D graphics that you can see on the screen.

Grind
To play through an area or section of a game over and over again to harvest loot or collect experience points and level up.

Indie game
Short for independent. A game created by a small team of developers—or even a single developer.

JRPG
Japanese role-playing game. A Japanese-made, role-playing game with the kind of gameplay and graphics you'd expect from a *Final Fantasy*, *Persona*, or *Dragon Quest* game.

Level
A portion or chapter of a game set in one area and with a beginning, an end, and a series of goals and challenges in-between.

Map
An in-game map to help you find objectives, or a level where players can fight in a multiplayer game.

MOBA
Multiplayer online battle arena. A multiplayer game where two teams of players select champions and go into battle for a series of objectives until one team wins.

Noob
A new and inexperienced player without the skills and knowledge of an experienced player.

NPC
Non-player character. A character in a game controlled by the computer. NPCs often provide help or guidance, sell goods, or help tell the story of the game.

The Legend of Zelda: Tears of the Kingdom

Open world
A style of game where players are free to explore one or more large areas and try out different activities, rather than complete one level after another.

Patch
An update to a game that fixes bugs or adds new features.

Platformer
Platform game. A type of game where you run across a series of platforms or a challenging landscape, leaping over gaps and obstacles, and avoiding or defeating enemies in your path.

Port
A version of a game made for one console or computer that's been converted to run on another.

PvE
Player vs. environment. An online game or game mode where players work together to beat computer-controlled enemies.

PvP
Player vs. player. An online game or game mode where players work against other players, either on their own or in teams.

Retro
A game or visual style that looks back to older games from the 1980s or 1990s.

Roguelike
A style of game where players fight through a series of randomly generated levels, killing monsters and collecting weapons and equipment.

RPG
Role-playing game. A type of game where the player goes on an epic quest or adventure, fighting monsters, leveling up, and upgrading their equipment along the way.

Song of Nunu: A League of Legends Story

Season pass
An add-on for a game that allows you to download and play through any expansions or DLC released after it launches.

Shoot-'em-up
A style of game based on classic arcade games, where players work their way through waves of levels full of enemies, blasting away at them and avoiding their attacks.

Speedrun
A gaming challenge where players compete to finish a game or level in the shortest possible time.

Streaming
Watching a video or playing a game through a live connection to the internet, rather than downloading it and then playing it from a console or computer.

VR
Virtual reality. Playing games through a head-mounted screen with motion controls, so that it looks and feels more like you're actually in the game world.

XP
Experience points. Points scored in a game for completing objectives, beating challenges, or killing monsters, and often used to upgrade the hero, their skills, or their equipment.